BLEAK HOUSE

A Novel of Connections

TWAYNE'S MASTERWORK STUDIES
Robert Lecker, General Editor

BLEAK HOUSE

A Novel of Connections

Norman Page

TWAYNE PUBLISHERS
A Division of G. K. Hall & Co. • Boston

Bleak House: A Novel of Connections

Twayne's Masterwork Studies No. 42

Copyright 1990 by G. K. Hall & Co.
All rights reserved.
Published by Twayne Publishers
A Division of G. K. Hall & Co.
70 Lincoln Street
Boston, Massachusetts 02111

Copyediting supervised by Barbara Sutton.
Book production by Janet Z. Reynolds.
Typeset in 10/14 Sabon
by Huron Valley Graphics, Ann Arbor, Michigan.

Printed on permanent/durable acid-free paper
and bound in the United States of America.

Library of Congress Cataloging-in-Publication Data

Page, Norman.
    Bleak House : a novel of connections / Norman Page.
        p.   cm.—(Twayne's masterwork studies ; no. 42)
    Includes bibliographical references.

    1. Dickens, Charles, 1812–1870. Bleak House. I. Title.
II. Series.
PR4556.P34 1990
823'.8—dc20   89-19782
                                                                CIP

ISBN 0-8057-8082-3 (alk. paper). 10 9 8 7 6 5 4 3 2 1
ISBN 0-8057-8128-5 (pbk. : alk. paper). 10 9 8 7 6 5 4 3 2 1
First published 1990.

For Brahma and Nandini Chaudhuri

Contents

Charles Dickens and his daughters.
Artist unknown.
Courtesy of the National Portrait Gallery, London.

Chronology:
Charles Dickens's Life and Works

1812   Charles John Huffam Dickens born 7 February at Portsea, Hampshire, second child and eldest son of John Dickens, clerk in the Navy Pay Office, and his wife, Elizabeth. A few months later family moves to a smaller and cheaper house in Portsea.

1814   Family moves to London.

1817   Family moves to Chatham, a naval dockyard in Kent, where Charles and his sister Fanny attend a dame school.

1822   Family moves back to London.

1824   Family's financial situation is desperate. Charles begins work at Warren's Blacking Warehouse, 9 February. John Dickens is arrested for debt and sent to the Marshalsea prison, late February. Elizabeth Dickens and younger children move into the prison, leaving Charles in lodgings. John Dickens is released, 28 May; shortly thereafter Charles leaves warehouse and attends Wellington House Academy.

1827   Leaves school and begins work in an attorney's office. Also learns shorthand.

1828   Becomes a free-lance shorthand reporter at Doctors' Commons (court abolished 1857).

1830   On his eighteenth birthday, applies for a reader's ticket at the British Museum. Visits the theater very frequently, takes lessons in acting, and has ambitions to become a professional actor.

1832   Becomes a reporter for *True Sun*, a new evening newspaper, and for *Mirror of Parliament*, a transcript of parliamentary proceedings.

1833   Begins to write fictional sketches of lower-class London life; his first published fiction, "A Dinner at Poplar Walk," appears in December.

1834   Becomes parliamentary reporter for *Morning Chronicle;* travels widely covering elections and political meetings. Continues to publish sketches. Uses pseudonym "Boz" for first time, August.

1835   Becomes engaged to Catherine Hogarth, April.

1836   *Sketches by Boz* published on his twenty-fourth birthday. First installment of *The Pickwick Papers* appears, 31 March; Dickens marries two days later. *Pickwick* becomes a huge popular success from the June number. Meets John Forster, Christmas Day.

1837   The first of his ten children is born, 6 January. Serialization of *Oliver Twist* in *Bentley's Miscellany*, of which Dickens is editor, begins in February. Serialization of *Pickwick* is completed in November. (It had appeared monthly, with an interruption in June after the death of seventeen-year-old Mary Hogarth, Dickens's sister-in-law, which left him prostrate with grief).

1838   Serialization of *Nicholas Nickleby* begins in April. *Oliver Twist* is published in volume form in November, but its serialization continues until April 1839.

1839   Leaves *Bentley's Miscellany* in February. Begins work on *Barnaby Rudge*.

1840   Publication of weekly magazine *Master Humphrey's Clock* begins, 4 April; serialization of *The Old Curiosity Shop* begins there, 25 April, continuing to 6 February 1841.

1841   Serialization of *Barnaby Rudge* begins on 13 February and continues to November. Visits Scotland in summer and is lionized in Edinburgh.

1842   With his wife, sets sail for the United States, 4 January; travels widely in the eastern states and in eastern Canada; returns to England in June. *American Notes* appears in October.

1843   Serialization of *Martin Chuzzlewit* begins in January and continues to June 1844. *A Christmas Carol* appears in December.

1844   Family (there are now five children) sets off for a year's residence in Italy, 2 July. *The Chimes*, second of the Christmas books, appears in December.

1845   Family returns to England in June. Another Christmas book, *The Cricket on the Hearth*, appears in December.

1846   Very briefly edits a new newspaper, the *Daily News*, 21 January to 9 February. *Pictures from Italy* appears in May. Family sets out for Switzerland, 31 May. Serialization of *Dombey and Son* begins in October. *The Battle of Life*, another Christmas book, is published in December.

1847   Family returns to London in March. Serialization of *Dombey* continues throughout year (ending in April 1848).

Chronology: Charles Dickens's Life and Works

1848   *The Haunted Man,* last of the series of Christmas books, appears in December.

1849   Serialization of *David Copperfield* begins in May.

1850   First issue of *Household Words,* a weekly magazine edited by Dickens, appears on 30 March. Continues as editor until 1859. Serialization of *David Copperfield* is concluded in November.

1851   Father dies, 31 March; baby daughter, Dora, dies two weeks later. Is busy with amateur theatricals throughout the year. Queen Victoria attends a performance of his production of Bulwer-Lytton's comedy *Not So Bad as We Seem* in May.

1852   Serialization of *Bleak House* begins in March.

1853   Finishes *Bleak House* in August; serialization is concluded in September. Sets out with two friends on an extended tour of France, Switzerland, and Italy in October; returns to England on 11 December. Reads *A Christmas Carol* in Birmingham for charity (the first of the public readings that were to dominate his later years) on 27 December.

1854   *Hard Times* appears serially in *Household Words* beginning 1 April, continuing to 12 August.

1855   Serialization of *Little Dorrit* begins in December. The family spends the winter in France.

1856   Family returns to France (to the seaside resort of Boulogne) for their summer holiday, June–August. Purchases Gad's Hill Place, near Rochester, Kent (a country house where he spends much of his time in his later years) in March.

1857   Serialization of *Little Dorrit* is completed in June. Meets a young actress, Ellen Ternan, in August.

1858   Gives the first of his public readings for profit, 29 April. Sixteen others follow during the next few weeks. Gives several hundred readings in Britain and America over the next dozen years. Separates from his wife in May. Gives ninety-one readings in the provinces, in Scotland and Ireland, and (over the Christmas season) in London in the later months of the year.

1859   Quarrels with the publishers of *Household Words* and resigns as editor. Launches a new weekly magazine, *All the Year Round,* on 30 April, on which date serialization of *A Tale of Two Cities* begins there, continuing to 26 November. Gives further readings in the provinces and in London in October and December.

1860   Serialization of *Great Expectations* in *All the Year Round* begins on 1 December, continuing to 3 August 1861.

1862	Undertakes an extensive provincial reading tour toward the end of the year; gives numerous other readings during the rest of the decade.
1863	Mother dies in September; son Walter (in India) dies in December.
1864	Serialization of *Our Mutual Friend,* his last completed novel, begins in May.
1865	Is involved in a serious railway accident, but is unhurt, in June; with him is Ellen Ternan, who has been his mistress for a considerable time. Serialization of *Our Mutual Friend* is completed in November.
1867	Arrives in Boston 19 November and begins a series of seventy-five readings in the United States the next month, continuing to 20 April 1868.
1868	Sails from New York on 22 April. Begins a tour of seventy-two readings in England, Scotland, and Ireland in October.
1869	Abandons his reading tour after a physical collapse and becomes seriously ill. Makes his will in May. Begins work on *The Mystery of Edwin Drood* in August.
1870	Gives his last public reading on 15 March. Serialization of *Drood* begins in April but novel is only half finished at his death on 9 June. Is buried in Westminster Abbey on 14 June.

1

Historical Context

Born in 1812, Charles Dickens was in his mid-twenties when Victoria came to the throne in 1837; by then he had already launched his brilliant career with the appearance of *The Pickwick Papers*, which began as a monthly serial on 31 March 1836. His childhood, adolescence, and young manhood were therefore pre-Victorian, as was his first hugely successful novel. But it is of course as a Victorian that we primarily think of Dickens—as the most popular novelist of his day, adored by a vast public, and ceaselessly (almost superhumanly) active until his untimely death in 1870.

As these dates suggest, his career almost exactly spans the first half of Victoria's reign. (The Queen herself was to survive until 1901, after the end of the nineteenth century.) It also coincides with a period of change and upheaval for which there had been no precedent in human history. Before Dickens's birth, the industrial revolution had begun to transform England from an agrarian to a predominantly urban society. The city as we know it, and in which most people in the western world now spend their lives, came into existence at about the time Dickens was born; soon afterward the landscape and, more profoundly, the whole pace and rhythm of life were permanently altered by the coming of the railways. In these respects and in many others, England was not only, in Disraeli's famous phrase, the workshop of the world; it was also the laboratory of the world, the place in which totally new developments were taking place.

Faced with new problems demanding urgent solutions, Dickens's England made some appalling mistakes—sometimes as a result of ignorance and inexperience, but often because of greed and indifference to the sufferings of others. The factory system, the city slums, the poverty, the lack of education and even of basic sanitation—the list could be continued for a long time. One of the great achievements of the nineteenth century was to remedy, through a series of legislative steps, the worst of these evils, but the remedies did not come quickly. Dickens was a passionate campaigner for reform, not only in his public speeches (he was reckoned one of the finest speakers of the day) and in his nonfictional writings (though he edited a popular magazine for twenty years) but in his immensely popular novels, read by almost every section of society.

Beginning in the 1830s, Dickens's career continued triumphantly through the 1860s. There were, however, important changes not only in his novels' construction and technique but in their mood during these decades. The early confidence and optimism gave way to something approaching gloom and despair. Perhaps this can be partly accounted for by the fact that he was no longer a young man, recently and happily married, with the world at his feet, but was middle-aged, unhappy in his personal life, and in deteriorating health. Beyond all this, though, the pessimism also seems a reaction to the problems of the age: a sense that they are so vast and pervasive as not to be open to easy solutions. For this reason the later novels have often been referred to as Dickens's "dark" novels, though it must quickly be added that the darkness does not exclude the comedy that is perhaps Dickens's greatest gift, nor his unceasing delight in human eccentricity.

Bleak House belongs almost exactly to the midpoint of Dickens's career: it was his ninth novel, and six more were to come, including the half-finished *Edwin Drood*. (As these figures indicate, his rate of production slowed down markedly as he grew older.) It can be regarded as the first of the "dark" novels. Opening, unforgettably, in the fog and mud of the London streets, it shows individuals struggling to live lives of love, duty, and compassion but constantly being faced—with sometimes tragic results—both by the selfishness of other individuals and by the workings of an impersonal system that seems beyond reform. The fog of the opening pages is both a physical reality and a symbol of the dense obscurities of the law; but the law itself is only an emblem or microcosm of a whole society that seems incapable of breaking free from the trammels of the past and moving into a brave new world of justice and equality.

It is quite natural to talk of "the world of Dickens," for his novels create a world that is as crowded, various, and surprising as the world most of us inhabit. *Bleak House* is a very long novel, and given its mode of publication, its length was a condition of its existence. There is also a sense, however, in which it could hardly have been any shorter, for it undertakes nothing less than the presentation of a comprehensive picture of a complex modern society. Later novelists were to attempt the same, but no one had done it before this time, so that in a sense Dickens invented a new kind of novel. It is something that was possible only because of the conjunction of his individual genius and the time at which he lived and wrote: the moment when the modern world, and modern society, were coming into existence.

COMPOSITION AND PUBLICATION

Dickens finished writing *David Copperfield* toward the end of October 1850: on the twenty-first of that month he wrote to his close friend John Forster that he was "within three pages" of the end and was "strongly divided, as usual in such cases, between sorrow and joy."[1] Serialization of the novel, which had begun a year and a half earlier, was completed in the following month. Thereupon Dickens, temporarily freed from the huge burden of producing the monthly installments of a long novel, threw himself with his characteristic energy into an entirely different activity. He had always had a passion for the theater, and before he became a writer he had thought seriously of becoming a professional actor. Now he exhanged the solitude of the author for the gregariousness of the strolling player, and in the closing months of 1850 and into the following year, amateur theatricals occupied much of his time and attention. With a group of friends he acted a leading role (needless to say) in Ben Jonson's comedy *Every Man in his Humour*. He told fellow novelist Edward Bulwer-Lytton on 3 November that he was to be regarded as "wholly at the disposal of the Theatricals until they shall be gloriously achieved," and later in the month he was able to report to another friend that they had gone off "in a whirl of triumph." After a sustained period of creative concentration, Dickens evidently needed the release afforded by this intensely practical activity.

But already a new novel was waiting to be born. As he wrote on 21 February 1851 after returning from a brief visit to Paris with two friends, "the first shadows of a new story" were "hovering in a ghostly way" about him. It was not, however, until much later in the year that he actually began to write *Bleak House*. Meanwhile, he was fully occupied. Editing his weekly magazine *Household Words* made constant demands on his attention; his theatrical activities also continued; and there were frequent requests for his services as an after-dinner speaker—a calling at which he excelled. For example, he spoke at the annual banquet of the Royal Academy on 3 May and at a dinner of the Metropolitan Sanitary Association (and sanitary reform, it is worth noting, is one of the issues dramatized in the soon-to-be-begun novel) a week later; in the following week he performed with his troupe of actors before the queen and the prince consort.

This prodigious level of activity was maintained despite personal griefs and anxieties. In March his wife Catherine, who seems to have been suffering from nervous strain, was placed under medical care at a considerable distance from London. Later in the month his father died after a painful illness. And only two weeks later his baby daughter Dora (named after an ill-fated character in *David Copperfield*) died at the age of seven months; Dickens spent the night sitting beside the child's body while John Forster traveled across England to break the news to Catherine and to bring her home.

Historical Context

Dickens's letters show evidence that, not long after these unhappy events, the new novel was slowly taking shape in his mind. He told Forster in August that he was "the victim of an intolerable restlessness," and at about the same time he wrote to another correspondent, "I begin to be pondering afar off, a new book. Violent restlessness and vague ideas of going I don't know where, I don't know why." Shortly afterward (on 7 September) he spoke of his next book as "waiting to be born," and a month later he described himself as "wild to begin a new book." It was less than a year since the completion of *Copperfield*; but Dickens was in his prime, and his imperious creative urge could be satisfied only by beginning a major new work. He evidently held discussions with his publishers, who during October announced that "a new serial work" by Dickens was shortly to appear. Readers in England and America—and the success of *Copperfield* had won him a large and loyal audience—looked forward eagerly to the new book, of which not a word had as yet been written.

It must, however, have been begun in November, for in a letter of 7 December he spoke of having only one more short chapter to write in order to complete the opening "number," or installment. The theatrical performances that had taken up so much of Dickens's time in recent months continued; in November the traveling actors appeared in the west of England, and while he was in Bath, Dickens called on veteran author Walter Savage Landor (who would serve as a model for Mr. Boythorn in *Bleak House*). As if all this were not enough, the Dickens family moved house: the larger home they now inhabited, in a fashionable area of London, reflected Dickens's growing success and prosperity.

On 1 March 1852 the first installment of the novel appeared, and the race to meet the monthly deadlines began once again. It was to be a long race, for the serialization of *Bleak House* would continue until September of the next year: twenty "numbers" would appear over nineteen consecutive months (the last a double number). Even without his other heavy commitments, the pressure on Dickens must have been enormous; but in his entire career he only once failed to meet the monthly deadline. That was when his beloved sister-in-law, Mary Hogarth, died during the simultaneous serialization of *Pickwick Papers* and *Oliver Twist,* and Dickens, crushed by grief and shock, was unable to meet his deadlines. The method of monthly serialization in twenty numbers had first been used for *Pickwick* and was followed for most, though not all, of Dickens's subsequent novels.

Dickens, who had recently (on 7 February) celebrated his fortieth birthday, was exhilarated by the initial success of *Bleak House.* Demand for the first number was so heavy on the day of publication that extra copies had to be printed that night. On 4 March he wrote to his father-in-law that the novel was "a great success" and was "blazing away merrily." Three days later he told Forster that the sales of the first number were "30,000 when I last heard." The initial printing had been twenty-five thousand copies, but evidently an additional five thousand had been called for; and by the end of June 38,500 copies of this opening number had been sold. In May Dickens wrote to a friend that the serial was "a most enormous success; all the prestige of Copperfield (which was very great) falling upon it, and raising its circulation above all my other books." He was not exaggerating. *David Copperfield* had had a circulation of under twenty-two thousand; the initial printing of the first number of *Bleak House,* as we have seen, exceeded this; and the figure rose steadily, to thirty-two thousand for the second number and thirty-four thousand for the third.

In the same letter to Forster, Dickens enclosed the proofs of the second number, due for publication some three weeks later. (He relied on Forster's critical judgment and often took his advice concerning his works in progress.) Clearly, at this stage of the serial run, Dickens was well ahead of his deadline, and no doubt he had ensured that when the serial began he would have a little in hand in case of emergency. Later, however, this leeway disappeared and the pressure began to mount. Nor was there much lessening in his multifarious other activities. *Household Words* continued to make its incessant demands on his time, and in August and September the strolling players toured the Midlands and the north of England. Family life also absorbed much of his energies: his tenth child had been born on 13 March, shortly after *Bleak House* began its run. His public speaking engagements continued to be numerous, and his time was also taken up both by his large circle of friends and by visitors who were welcomed and shown the sights. In May 1853, for example, two American visitors to London spent time with Dickens: Harriet Beecher Stowe, author of *Uncle Tom's Cabin,* and Cornelius Felton, a Harvard professor whom he had met and liked during his tour of America in 1842.

So work on the novel continued throughout 1852 and into the following year. On 7 Febraury 1853 Dickens wrote to his friend Dr. John Elliotson, a distinguished physician, thanking him for the loan of his "remarkable and learned Lecture on Spontaneous Combustion." The *Bleak House* character Krook had perished of "Spontaneous Combustion" in the tenth number of the novel, published in December 1852, and the episode had sparked off a controversy between Dickens and G. H. Lewes, scientist and man of letters, concerning the scientific possibility or impossibility of such a death.

Early in June 1853 Dickens fell ill and, very unusually for him, spent six days confined to his bed. On recovering he decided that he needed a complete change, and later in the month he traveled with his wife and sister-in-law to Boulogne, a French seaside town, where he had leased a holiday house. His health was soon completely restored, and work on the novel was resumed. On 18 June he reported himself as at work on the seventeenth number, which was finished five days later. (This number contains chapters 54–56, narrating the flight of Lady Dedlock.) On 29 June he sent to his illustrator, H. K. Browne, suggestions for the illustrations to appear in the eighteenth number; at the same time he promised that the subjects for the illustrations in the final double number would be sent within a day or two. This is clear evidence that Dickens was ready to begin the creative dash that would take him to the finish line, exhausted but triumphant, and that (since the choice of illustrations emphasized the main themes of the number) he had a definite notion of what the closing chapters would contain. Less than a month later he wrote to another friend, the actor W. C. Macready, that he had been working hard at *Bleak House* since arriving in Boulogne and that, after a week's rest, he was now setting to work to finish the final number. On 5 August he was "just getting fairly into" the conclusion of the novel; three weeks later, on 25 August, he read the final installment to his family and wrote to a friend, with obvious gratification, that it had made a "great impression" on them.

The final stages of composition had, as usual, been very arduous: Dickens told one friend that he had been "very hard at work" since arriving in Boulogne, "often getting up at daybreak to write through many hours." The last installment of the novel appeared at the beginning of September, and the entire novel, with a preface added, was published in volume form at about the same time.

What has been said so far indicates quite clearly that the problems of writing a serial novel, in the particular circumstances in which Dickens chose to work, were very different from those encountered by other novelists; and these are questions that need to be explored more closely, since they had a profound influence on the kind of work that *Bleak House* turned out to be. Moreover, for readers as well as for the author of such a novel, the experience was a highly distinctive one. The first readers of *Bleak House* did not, as we do, hold the entire novel in their hands, enjoy complete freedom to read it as rapidly as they wished, or even, if they choose, have the power to look at the end long before they reach it. Instead, they received the novel in portions—usually three chapters a month, sometimes four, making up a "number"—and, having read the monthly portion, had to contain their impatience to read on, for the very good reason that what came next was not only not yet published but probably not yet written!

Reading a long novel over a long period of time (more than a year and a half) placed a considerable burden on the reader's memory, since knowledge of both the intricacies of the plot and of the large cast of characters had to be retained if the later numbers were to be understood and enjoyed. As we shall see, this led the novelist to modify his conception of plot and character in ways that aided the reader's memory. Each number had to satisfy certain requirements: to remind the reader of what had gone before, to advance the story significantly, to hold out promises of what was still to come, and to be satisfying in itself. No wonder that not all novelists in the Victorian period found the serial novel a congenial vehicle for their art. George Eliot, for instance, whose method is much more leisurely and analytic than the concentrated, highly dramatic mode of Dickens, preferred to work in much longer units: *Middlemarch,* which is about the same length as *Bleak House,* originally appeared in eight installments, each of which was of course much longer than the monthly portions of Dickens's novel.

There can be no doubt, however, that Dickens found serialization stimulating as well as lucrative. (Its main attraction for the professional novelist was that it ensured a double profit, first from the serial, then from the entire novel published in volume form.) Perhaps above all, he relished the sense of closeness to his audience that serialization provided. Instead of having to wait to see how his completed novel would be received—by which time the creative passion had died down, and the writer might well have lost interest in his work—he could receive, and even respond to, the reactions of both professional critics (for individual numbers of serialized novels were sometimes reviewed) and private readers. Dickens had recently experienced this in December 1849, when he received a letter from a Mrs. Seymour Hill. She had been upset to recognize herself portrayed as the grotesque and unattractive figure of Miss Mowcher in *David Copperfield.* Overcome by remorse as a result of Mrs. Hill's complaint, he changed his intentions with regard to this character. On the other hand, at the beginning of 1841, when serialization of *The Old Curiosity Shop* was drawing to an end, Dickens firmly resisted all pleas to spare the life of his heroine Little Nell (though he was surely gratified to receive them as a tribute to his own power).

A serial novelist was also necessarily sensitive to the month-by-month sales of his novel in progress, for the audience was by no means a captive one and could simply stop buying the monthly numbers if the novel failed to hold their interest. Again, in the 1840s, Dickens had been disappointed by the early sales of *Martin Chuzzlewit* as it appeared monthly; his sudden decision to give the story a new interest by sending his hero to America added about two thousand to the monthly sales.

If we try to reconstruct the experience of the reader of 1852–53 who encounters "Mr. Dickens's new novel" as it appears, then, it is an experience different in many important ways from our own in reading, say, a modern paperback reprint. At the beginning of each month the eager reader could go to a bookshop and purchase the latest number for one shilling. (If he did so throughout the entire nineteen months, he would possess the whole novel and could, if he wished, have the separate parts stripped of their covers and advertisements and bound together.) What he received was a paper-covered booklet containing thirty-two pages of text and a couple of illustrations. As already indicated, each number contained three or four chapters. In the Penguin edition of *Bleak House* the end of a number is indicated; thus the first number (March 1852) comprises the first four chapters, the second number (April 1852) takes the reader to the end of chapter 7, and so on. It is interesting and instructive to read the novel with these divisions in mind and to consider the integrity and coherence of individual numbers and other related questions. Which characters are given a rest and left unmentioned for one or more numbers? How is each number apportioned between the two narrators? And is it really true, as it is sometimes claimed, that Dickens felt an obligation to end every number at a moment of cliff-hanging suspense or with a dramatic climax? (A glance at the end of the opening number quickly explodes that particular myth.)

A word needs to be said about the illustrations that accompanied each number. A selection of these is included in most modern editions, but it is worth finding an edition that includes them all; for in a real sense *Bleak House* is an illustrated novel, and the interaction of text and picture is a significant element in the total meaning. We know from his letters and other evidence that Dickens took a keen interest in the illustrations and closely supervised their execution, so it is only reasonable to regard them as further revealing his intentions as a novelist. His illustrator for *Bleak House* was Hablôt K. Browne, who had worked for him ever since the early days of *Pickwick* and had adopted the pseudonym "Phiz" in imitation of Dickens's own pen name "Boz." Browne produced a total of thirty-eight etchings for this novel, and in addition, he made a woodcut that was used as a cover design for each monthly number. The latter is well worth careful examination as it embodies, sometimes symbolically or allegorically, many of the main motifs of the novel and indicates how clear Dickens's intentions were from the outset.[2]

It has often been said that our mental images of Dickens's scenes and characters owe much to his illustrators, of whom Browne was by far the most important; but it must also be added that Dickens did not give them a free hand but kept a close eye on their work, proposing subjects for illustration, insisting on modifications when their sketches did not accurately reflect his conceptions, and sometimes rejecting them outright. A typical letter to Browne was written from Boulogne on 29 July 1853. In it Dickens enclosed "the subjects for the next No." and asks Browne to "let me see the sketches here by post": in other words, he gave instructions as to which scenes from the number were to be illustrated and indicated that the artist's preliminary sketches were to be sent for his approval or criticism. It was hardly a partnership of equals, but this strengthens the case for regarding the illustrations as an essential element in the work that we call *Bleak House*—and even for arguing that an edition that leaves them out, or a reading that ignores them, is incomplete.

There is no evidence that Dickens's early novels, such as *Pickwick Papers* and *Nicholas Nickleby*, were carefully planned. Dickens seems to have relied upon his incredible energy and unlimited powers of invention to carry him along, and the construction of these works is loose and episodic. From *Dombey and Son* (serialized in 1846–48) onward, however, his conception of the novel changed in a way that demanded much more careful planning. His aim was to present a picture of society with great richness of detail and variety of character and scene and incident, but at the same time to ensure that everything illustrated the novel's central theme and that there were innumerable interconnections among the different parts. Such a novel could not have been written in a spirit of improvisation, and Dickens devised a method that served him well, for he continued to use it to the end of his career. This was to make notes or memoranda, often referred to as "number-plans," that enabled him to plan each installment carefully and to ensure that the various strands of the story and groups of characters were kept under control. Fortunately these notes have survived and are kept, with the manuscript and corrected proofs of the novel (and with most of Dickens's other major manuscripts), in the Forster Collection at London's Victoria and Albert Museum.

It quickly becomes clear that Dickens made two kinds of notes. (His practice was to fold a piece of paper down the middle and to make one kind on one side, the other on the other.) One kind became part of a reservoir of ideas that could sooner or later be drawn on: names of characters to be introduced, very brief summaries of incidents to be narrated, hints of recurring themes and motifs to be developed, even snatches of dialogue later to be expanded into full-length speeches or conversations. As the novel developed and Dickens had to keep more and more areas of interest going, one of his problems was what can be included and what he could afford to leave out until next time; these notes provide fascinating glimpses of his creative dilemmas and decisions. The notes for the seventh number include, among other items, the following (Dickens's system of underlining is not reproduced here):

Mr. Guppy—His mother? Not yet
Mr. Krook Yes
The Turveydrops. No. Next time . . .
The Brickmaker's family? Slightly
Gridley? Very slightly
Mr. Tulkinghorn? Carry on[3]

The same half-sheet contains some notes headed "mems: [memoranda] for future," beginning: "Mr. Tulkinghorn finds Joe—hearing from Mr. Snagsby what he said there—and gets him to identify Lady Dedlock. . . ." Such jottings seem to suggest that Dickens was anxious to clarify in his own mind the complexities of the plot. Presumably he made these notes before he began to write the number, adding to them as he went along, and found them useful both as a guide in the process of composition and to refer back to at later stages.

The other kind of note Dickens made, on the right-hand side of his sheet of paper, indicated the division of his material into the chapters that would constitute the number. Here he usually gave the numbers and titles of the chapters, together with some indication of their contents. Thus the notes for chapter 31, "Nurse and Patient," sketch in the barest outline the stages of the action in this important chapter, and conclude, interestingly, with two scraps of dialogue to be used at the emotional climaxes of the final episode:

> JO begin the illnesses from him. His disappearance
> Then, Charley ill
> Then, Esther
> Ada
> "She will try to make her way into the room. Keep her out!"
> "For I cannot see you Charley—I am blind" (944)

Laconic as this is, it was sufficient for Dickens, who had no doubt enacted the scene in his imagination and, like an actor, needed only these cue words in order to reproduce it in full.

Not surprisingly, Dickens's notes became more numerous as his novel neared its conclusion and he was faced with the daunting tasks both of bringing his narrative to a conclusion and of bringing on nearly all his characters for a final appearance, however brief, like actors bidding farewell to the audience that has been watching them for so long.

Dickens's notes for *Bleak House* yield one other suggestive body of information, this one relating to the title of the novel. Names of books and characters were of great importance to Dickens, and he liked to settle them before he started (though he was prepared to change them later if they failed to strike him as exactly right). On ten separate sheets of paper he wrote down projected titles for this novel, and it is only on the final sheet that he arrived at the one by which the novel became known. His first idea was *Tom-all-Alone's*, which may seem surprising but demands that the role of the notorious London slum in the story be carefully assessed. *The Ruined House, The Solitary House,* and *The East Wind* are also titles that were considered and rejected. Predictably, Chancery makes an appearance in several of those written down. We may be sure that *Bleak House* eventually struck Dickens with a sense of its absolute rightness, and its appropriateness therefore needs to be given the serious attention it deserves. It must have taken not a little courage to use a title that many readers, accustomed to thinking of Dickens as primarily a humorist and an entertainer, would have found disconcerting and even uninviting.

2

The Importance of the Work

It is worth remembering that *Bleak House* is only one work (though a very important one) in a long list of classic novels that appeared during the decade from 1847 to 1857, in the middle of which Dickens's novel was written and published. Those years also saw the appearance of Charlotte Brontë's *Jane Eyre* (1847), *Shirley* (1849), and *Villette* (1857); Emily Brontë's *Wuthering Heights* (1847); Ann Brontë's *The Tenant of Wildfell Hall* (1848); Thackeray's *Vanity Fair* (1848), *Pendennis* (1849), and *Henry Esmond* (1852); Elizabeth Gaskell's *Mary Barton* (1848), *Ruth* (1853), and *Cranford* (1853); Anthony Trollope's *The Warden* (1855) and *Barchester Towers* (1857); George Eliot's *Scenes of Clerical Life* (1857); and four other major novels by Dickens: *Dombey and Son* (1848), *David Copperfield* (1850), *Hard Times* (1854), and *Little Dorrit* (1857). This list of nearly twenty titles by no means exhausts the catalog of novels that survive from the hundreds that appeared during those years.

Clearly it was a period of extraordinary flowering for the English novel: there are few decades, in any period, that rival this short span of time for richness and variety in fiction. (Nothing has been said of the poetic productions of the same years, but it may just be mentioned that

1847–57 also saw the publication of the most famous poem of the Victorian age, Tennyson's *In Memoriam* (1850) and of Browning's most important volume, *Men and Women* (1854). It was also, incidentally, a period of great vitality in the American novel, during which such classics as Hawthorne's *The Scarlet Letter* (1850), Harriet Beecher Stowe's *Uncle Tom's Cabin* (1852), and much of Melville's best work, including *Moby-Dick* (1851), appeared.) As for Dickens, the period saw the full maturing of his art, and *Bleak House* is one of the most important productions of his middle years.

This was, then, a time when the novel flourished in England as never before, with the result that it became in the course of the second half of the nineteenth century the dominant literary form. Central to this achievement was Dickens, whose career as a novelist was hugely successful and whose death in 1870 left a gap that was never really filled. A few years before *Bleak House*, he had had his first major commercial success with *Dombey and Son*, the sales figures for which convey some notion of his great popularity. The first printing of the first monthly installment of *Dombey* was of twenty-five thousand copies, and it sold out within hours of its appearance. Printings of later numbers rose to thirty-three thousand and even higher. It should be remembered that each number was read by several people, so that a considerable proportion of the literate population was following the story as it came from Dickens's pen. His total profits on the serial were in excess of nine thousand pounds, a sum roughly equivalent (taking into account the currency value during the period) to between one-quarter and one-half a million dollars. By comparison, Thackeray's *Vanity Fair*, which was appearing simultaneously, achieved a sale of fewer than five thousand copies per number, and Thackeray was paid a mere sixty pounds for each installment. *Bleak House* was even more successful than *Dombey:* on the day that he completed it, Dickens wrote to a friend, "I have never had so many readers," and he repeated the boast in the preface he added to the novel when it appeared in volume form ("I believe I have never had so many readers as in this book").

In at least two respects *Bleak House* differs from the novels by his contemporaries listed at the beginning of this chapter—it differs in being more ambitious in its conception and in being more boldly innovative in its methods. Let me say a little about each of these claims, though both will be developed more fully in the chapters that follow. Charlotte Brontë showed a profound insight into the inner life of the individual and the development of selfhood; Emily Brontë showed the destructive power of human passion; Thackeray analyzed the changing structure of English society; Elizabeth Gaskell exposed the misery and hardships suffered by the poor. Dickens touched on all of these and much else, but he also undertook something that none of the others attempted or even contemplated doing, and that was to give a full picture of English society and a revelation of what it is that keeps people apart and binds them together. This was a grander conception, and a grander achievement, than that of any other Victorian novelist; for parallels we have to go to the great European masters such as Balzac and Tolstoy.

But it is not only the ideas and the feelings that generate this great novel that place it in a class apart from the work of Dickens's contemporaries. In form and technique it is startlingly original and "modern"—intricate in its design and relating small details to overall patterns. It is unique even in Dickens's own work for its experimental handling of narrative technique and point of view.

In studying *Bleak House*, therefore, we are studying not only a text by a famous author, but one of the finest achievements of England's greatest novelist and, even more than this, a work that enlarged the boundaries of fiction. After *Bleak House* the novel was never quite the same again, and it is not surprising to find that one of the pioneers of modernist fiction, Joseph Conrad, read and reread it and in his own practice demonstrably learned from it.

3

Critical Reception

Produced almost exactly at the midpoint of Dickens's career, *Bleak House* is evaluated by the modern reader in relation to his novels that followed it as well as those that preceded it. Thus Barbara Hardy argues that it initiated a series of "novels of the sociological imagination" that "set out a full map and large-scale criticism, in the expressive form of art, of Dickens's England,"[4] and Philip Collins suggests that it is "a crucial item in the history of Dickens's reputation."[5] It is important to remember, however, that the first readers of *Bleak House* could relate it only to the works that had preceded it, and their reactions must be judged in this light.

Characteristic of many readers who were Dickens's contemporaries is a reviewer in *The Rambler* who referred to Dickens as "the author of the *Pickwick Papers*," praised him as "An unrivalled humorist, and eminently respectable in his morals," but observed regretfully of this latest novel that "his knowledge of human nature is as superficial as it is extensive."[6] This is clearly a very different view of the novel from Barbara Hardy's; but then the contemporary reviewer, unlike the modern critic, could not have approached *Bleak House* as the first of a series of masterpieces in which the novelist undertook a comprehensive exposure of the condition of mid-Victorian England. Instead, the contemporary reviewer saw the novel as evidence of a disappointing reluctance on Dickens's part to repeat his earlier successes. For the reader of Dickens's own generation he was preeminently "the author of *The Pickwick Papers*" and its successors, including *Nicholas Nickleby, The Old Curiosity Shop,* and *Martin Chuzzlewit,* in which comedy and sentiment are paramount. The novels of the 1850s and 1860s, on the other hand, are darker and more uncompromising in their diagnoses of the ills of the age. It is precisely the later Dickens that many modern critics have come to esteem most highly. Hence the discrepancy between contemporary and later views of *Bleak House,* neatly summed up by Philip Collins: "For many critics in the 1850s, '60s, and '70s, [*Bleak House*] began the drear decline of 'the author of *Pickwick, Chuzzlewit* and *Copperfield*'; for many recent critics—anticipated by G. B. Shaw—it opened the greatest phase of his achievement."[7]

The reactions of the novel's first readers can best be described as mixed. Charlotte Brontë must have read the first number almost as soon as it appeared, for on 11 March 1852 she wrote to George Smith that she "liked the Chancery part" but found Esther Summerson's narrative "weak and twaddling." (She could hardly have avoided comparing Esther with her own Jane Eyre, who had burst upon the world five years earlier.) A few days later the critic Henry Crabb Robinson noted in his diary that he had read the first number and had found that it "does not promise much, except an exposure of the abuses of Chancery practice." Later entries in Robinson's diary show that he enjoyed such characters as Jarndyce, Skimpole, and Boythorn but had strong reservations about the book's overall success; the fifth number, for instance, was read "without any pleasure."[8]

No less mixed were the public verdicts of the reviewers when the novel eventually appeared in volume form. "*Bleak House* is, in some respects, the worst of Mr Dickens' fictions," declared one, "but, in many more, it is the best." The anonymous reviewer in *Bentley's Miscellany* (a magazine of which Dickens himself had at one time been editor) deplored its "tendency to disagreeable exaggeration," which was more "conspicuous" than in any of Dickens's earlier books. A similar opinion was expressed by the influential critic H. F. Chorley, who wrote, "There is progress in art to be praised in this book—and there is progress in exaggeration to be deprecated," while yet another critic, George Brimley, commented more fully on the same charge of "exaggeration": "The love of strong effect, and the habit of seizing peculiarities and presenting them instead of characters, pervade Mr Dickens's gravest and most amiable portraits, as well as those expressly intended to be ridiculous and grotesque." For the reviewer in *Bentley's*, "grotesque" was a term of disapproval: registering surprise at "the almost entire absence of humour" in the novel (another instance of judging *Bleak House* by criteria derived from Dickens's earlier work), he insisted that "the grotesque and the contemptible have taken the place of the humorous."[9]

Some individual characters, on the other hand, elicited high praise. Jo the crossing-sweeper was a particular favourite. Chorley, who complained that some of the characters, including Mr. Snagsby, relied too much on mannerisms that became tedious through repetition ("The queerest catch-word may be used too mercilessly, even for a farce—much more for a novel"), found Jo a shining exception: "Perhaps among all the waifs and strays, the beggars and the outcasts, in behalf of whose humanity our author has again and again appealed to a world too apt to forget their existence, he has never produced anything more rueful, more pitiable, more complete than poor Jo. The dying scene, with its terrible morals and impetuous protest, Mr Dickens has nowhere in all his works excelled."[10] Another distinguished reader, Dean Ramsay, went even further in stating that nothing in English fiction surpassed the death of Jo. For different reasons, Inspector Bucket was also widely praised: for the *Bentley's* reviewer he was "a portrait that stands out from the canvas just like a bit of life," while Brimley also paid tribute to Bucket's authenticity, noting that "he bears evidence of the careful study of this admirable department of our Police by the editor of *Household Words*." The modern reader may be less ready to share Brimley's enthusiasm for Boythorn ("one of the most original and happiest conceptions of the book, a humorist study of the highest merit"), though Brimley himself was less enthusiastic about Tulkinghorn ('his motives and character are quite incomprehensible").[11] As these examples suggest, Victorian reviewers tended to respond to characters individually rather than to consider their relationship to each other and to the central themes of the novel. It is a little startling to find the *Bentley's* reviewer demanding, "Of what conceivable use . . . is such a personage as Mr Harold Skimpole?,"[12] since Skimpole's selfishness so clearly links him to other characters in a complex pattern of parallels and contrasts.

This failure to perceive the underlying pattern or design of Dickens's novel led some contemporary reviewers to make the surprising judgment that *Bleak House* is lacking in story or plot. Brimley found in it an "absolute want of construction" (not a judgment that many modern critics are prepared to endorse) and stated, "The great Chancery suit of Jarndyce and Jarndyce, which serves to introduce a crowd of persons as suitors, lawyers, law-writers, law-stationers, and general spectators of Chancery business, has positively not the smallest influence on the character of any one person concerned, nor has it any interest of itself." Another reviewer complained that the "one grand defect" of the novel was that "Mr Dickens fails in the construction of a plot. . . . He resorts to a thousand artifices to excite curiosity; and lo! there is nothing about which we need have been curious—there is no explanation by which, when our curiosity has been excited, it will be gratified or satisfied."[13] Again, we are unlikely to share such opinions, but Dickens's contemporaries did not of course share our knowledge of the very careful planning that went into the book, of which the number-plans provide evidence. Nor did they enjoy the benefit of the hindsight that enables us to see *Bleak House* as one of the earliest of the novels in which a central theme and an inclusive design are of overriding importance. Significantly, it was Dickens's close friend John Forster who actually used the term *design* in his review of this novel in the *Examiner:* praising the descriptions of Chesney Wold "throughout the tale," he suggested that they not only "have great beauty in themselves" but "are so employed as to bear always a subtle and thoughtful reference to the imaginative and romantic design of the story."[14] (Forster's epithet "romantic" perhaps echoed Dickens's own statement in the preface to the first edition that he had "purposely dwelt upon the romantic side of familiar things.") Since Forster was in closer touch than anyone else with Dickens's creative ideas at this stage of his career, it seems likely that his observations have behind them the authority of Dickens's own convictions and intentions.

Two of Dickens's well-known contemporaries took exception to specific elements in the novel. John Stuart Mill complained indignantly that Dickens had had "the vulgar impudence . . . to ridicule rights of women" in his satirical portrait of Mrs. Jellyby—a response that led Mill to regard *Bleak House* as "much the worst of his things, and the only one of them I altogether dislike." Even more revealing is George Henry Lewes's sustained attack on the episode in chapter 32 in which Krook perishes of "Spontaneous Combustion": "according to all known chemical and physiological laws," wrote Lewes, "Spontaneous Combustion is an *impossibility*."[15] Dickens's daring symbolic art and Lewes's concern for scientific accuracy met in a head-on collision; the interesting thing is that, rather than defending the episode in terms of its symbolic rightness, Dickens insisted in his preface that there are numerous authenticated cases of spontaneous combustion that are matters of historical record ("I do not wilfully or negligently mislead my readers" [42]).

Most professional critics of Dickens's day, then, saw *Bleak House* in very different ways from the modern reader: their judgments of such matters as construction and character often seem to have missed the point, and they paid little or no attention to aspects that seem to us of crucial importance (for example, the experimental narrative method and the use of pervading symbols). In the decades immediately following Dickens's death in 1870, his reputation as a whole suffered a severe decline: in 1883 he was characterized in Anthony Trollope's posthumously published autobiography as "Mr Popular Sentiment," and five years later the influential critic Leslie Stephen referred to him patronizingly (in the *Dictionary of National Biography*) as a writer enjoying a "popularity with the half-educated." A verdict on *Bleak House* typical of this stage of its critical history was offered by A. W. Ward, who in 1882 contributed a volume on Dickens to Stephen's popular English Men of Letters series. Ward was shrewd enough to be aware that in *Bleak House* Dickens had attempted something new: "Dickens . . . for the first time emancipated himself from that form of novel which, in accordance with his great eighteenth century favourites, he had hitherto more or less consciously adopted—the novel of adventure, of which the person of the hero, rather than the machinery of the plot, forms the connecting element." Yet Ward seems unaware that this was the source of great strength and power and of new possibilities for the novel. He concluded:

> With all its merits, *Bleak House* has little of that charm which belongs to so many of Dickens' earlier stories, and to *David Copperfield* above all. In part at least, this may be due to the excessive severity of the task which Dickens had set himself in *Bleak House;* for hardly any other of his works is constructed on so large a scale, or contains so many characters organically connected with the progress of its plot; and in part, again, to the half-didactic half-satirical purport of the story, which weighs heavily on the writer.[16]

The modern critic is unlikely to share either Ward's criteria or his critical vocabulary: the very title of the novel warns us not to expect "charm." What is most striking about this late-Victorian assessment is that it deplored the very qualities that later critics have praised: the grandiose conception, the panoramic portrayal of society, the power and passion of the satire, the intricacy of the construction, and the cross-references.

In 1911, a generation after Ward, G. K. Chesterton came closer to a modern reading of *Bleak House* when he observed that "the whole tale is symbolic and crowded with symbols. Miss Flite is a funny character, like Miss La Creevy [in *Nicholas Nickleby*], but Miss La Creevy means only Miss La Creevy, Miss Flite means Chancery."[17] But another generation passed before the greatness of *Bleak House* began to be fully recognized, as part of the rehabilitation of Dickens some seventy years after his death. In 1939, in his classic essay "Dickens: The Two Scrooges," Edmund Wilson described the novel as "the masterpiece of [Dickens's] middle period" and argued, "it is one of Dick-

ens' victories in his rapid development as an artist that he should
succeed in transforming his melodramatic intrigues of stolen inheri-
tances, lost heirs and ruined maidens—with their denunciatory con-
frontations that always evoke the sound of fiddling in the orchestra—
into devices of artistic dignity. Henceforth the solution of the mystery
is to be also the moral of the story and the last word of Dickens' social
'message.' "[18] At almost exactly the same time on the other side of the
Atlantic, George Orwell, in another classic essay that was to be widely
influential, declared, "In *Oliver Twist, Hard Times, Bleak House, Little Dorrit,* Dickens attacked English institutions with a ferocity that
has never since been approached."[19] Dickens criticism had come a
long way from his contemporaries' preoccupation with character and
Ward's emphasis on charm.

In the last half century, Dickens has come to be widely recognized
as the greatest of English novelists, and *Bleak House* as one of the
greatest of his achievements. It has also received an unprecedented
share of critical attention. In his authoritative survey of recent Dickens
criticism, Philip Collins notes that it has been "the most written about
of the novels."[20] Barbara Hardy begins her monograph on Dickens's
later novels with *Bleak House* and thus endorses the view of it as
representing a new and important departure in Dickens's career; for
her, the title points forward to the later masterpieces that "explore
more bleakly a bleaker world."[21]

A READING

4

The Topicality of
Bleak House

On 1 May 1851 the Great Exhibition opened in the Crystal Palace, an astonishing edifice of iron and glass that had risen in Hyde Park. The exhibition was both a celebration of and an advertisement for Britain's material prosperity and its mechanical and technological achievements—a vast and crowded justification of the country's claim to be the workshop of the world. Dickens went twice, but did not share the general enthusiasm. As we have seen, it was at this time that *Bleak House* (as yet unnamed) was beginning to haunt his creative mind and to demand to be written. The novel would depict England in terms almost exactly the opposite of those implicit in the idea of the exhibition. Dickens found little to celebrate and much to deplore there, little cause for complacency but a great deal of cause for anger and sadness.

The sense of being at odds with the prevailing mood of the age—or at any rate with the mood of the governing class and the prosperous bourgeoisie—was nothing new for Dickens. At the beginning of 1851 he had written for *Household Words* an article entitled "The Last Words of the Old Year" in which the dying year, personified, looks back at the grimmer aspects of the period ("forty-five persons in every hundred are found to be incapable of reading or writing; starving children who stole a loaf out of a baker's shop have been sentenced to be whipped in the House of Correction . . .") and looks forward to the forthcoming exhibition:

> I have seen a project carried into execution for a great assemblage of the peaceful glories of the world. I have seen a wonderful structure, reared in glass, by the energy and skill of a great natural genius [Joseph Paxton], self-improved: worthy descendant of my Saxon ancestors: worthy type of ingenuity triumphant! Which of my children shall behold the Princes, Prelates, Nobles, Merchants, of England, equally united, for another Exhibition—for a great display of England's sins and negligences, to be, by steady contemplation of all eyes, and steady union of all hearts and hands, set right? (4 January 1851)

It is that other exhibition, displaying "England's sins and negligences," that he sets before the readers of *Bleak House*. One reviewer of the complete novel was to remark in *Bentley's Monthly Review* (October 1853) that "Mr Dickens always writes *with a purpose* now." More precisely, though, it is a novel with many purposes, and this chapter explores the most important of them.

Philip Collins has observed of Dickens's work in general that "more of his jokes and social references than is often realized were right up-to-date, concerned with events, issues and personalities prominent in the previous month or so."[22] As this suggests, one feature of serial publication was that it enabled the writer whose composition was very close to the date of publication to incorporate references to topics that his readers would very recently have encountered in their newspapers or in a satirical journal such as *Punch*. It is sometimes supposed that Dickens acted as a kind of investigative journalist, using his novels to bring to public attention matters hitherto unknown or ignored. Much more often, however, he seems to have used his art to intensify his readers' reactions to issues that were already in the public domain. As Humphry House says, "Both the Court of Chancery and the slums were topical subjects in 1852, for other reasons than because

Dickens made them so. People were then in fact dying of litigation and of cholera."[23] His contemporaries were sometimes ready to make the same point: as a critic discussing *Bleak House* in the *Eclectic Review* (December 1853) put it, Dickens "only exhibits in a stronger and more romantic light what has been pretty well made known before through the earnest prose of plainer men."

There is, however, a problem with the topicality of the novel. As House points out, "Dickens seems to have gone out of his way to leave the imaginary time of the story vague": though the reader has a strong sense of the sequence of events and of time passing, there are almost no indications of time, apart from the changing seasons and law-court terms—no year is ever mentioned (Esther actually says "I omit the date") and "there is scarcely even the name of a month."[24] Paradoxically, therefore, a novel that has in so many aspects the unmistakable feel of contemporaneity is also free floating in a timeless, or at any rate a vague early-Victorian or even pre-Victorian, setting.

Esther's narrative is retrospective, and near the end she tells us that she is writing "full seven years" after the conclusion of the action. Since in the course of the action Esther herself grows from childhood to womanhood, and since, as House says, "from Esther's first going to Bleak House to the death of Richard was something just less than three years,"[25] the story of Esther's childhood must open in the 1830s or earlier, and the main action must be set in the mid-1840s at the latest. But these dates are inconsistent with one or two specific references to events of an earlier date and many more that are much closer to the date of composition. For example, the "Spanish refugees" mentioned in passing in chapter 43 as a feature of the Somers Town district of London belong to the 1820s and seem to be a nostalgic and self-indulgent recollection of Dickens's childhood in that area. They belong to an entirely different generation from the mid-century figure of Bucket the detective or from the topical issues already mentioned and those discussed below in more detail.

The most obvious explanation is that Dickens was not greatly concerned with chronological consistency and was certainly not prepared to sacrifice a telling local effect to such considerations. As

House says, much of the legal world of the book, especially the depiction of the shabby inhabitants of lawyers' offices, was "drawn out of the inexhaustible store of memories from Dickens's early days."[26] (Perhaps Guppy was in part even a self-mocking portrait of the artist as a young man.) But overlaying this evocation of the past was "a reformist's anger with the immediate present" that led Dickens to engage himself with the highly topical issues that his first readers would have recognized.

Dickens had worked in a lawyer's office as a very young man, and as a shorthand reporter he had seen the courts in action—or inaction. In 1844 he had tried unsuccessfully to stop an unauthorized edition of one of his books and had become involved in the expense and frustration of a suit in the Court of Chancery. Nearer the date of the novel, in 1850 and 1851, he had published in *Household Words* two articles titled "The Martyrs in Chancery." And in "The Last Words of the Old Year" referred to above he had commented on the legacy of the old year to the new, the Court of Chancery, "The less he leaves of it to his successor, the better for mankind" (4 January 1851). By this time, and long before he began working on *Bleak House,* the evils of Chancery and the move to reform it had become matters of public discussion. In a valuable essay in *Dickens at Work* (from which I also take the title of this chapter) John Butt refers to "the interest which everyone was taking in chancery" in 1851.[27] On the first day of that year the *Times* had published a leading article on the subject, attacking "the *inertia* of an antiquated jurisprudence and the obstacles raised by personal or professional interest." A week earlier another article had attacked the question less abstractly and in terms that anticipate the novel: "If a house be seen in a peculiarly dilapidated condition, the beholder at once exclaims, 'Surely that property must be in Chancery.'. . . the lingering and expectant suitors waste their lives as well as their substance in vain hopes, and death robs them of their wished-for triumph, if ruin have not already rendered it impossible." Dickens's projected title for his novel, "The Ruined House," seems to echo this passage.

Butt summarizes, "In December and January alone the columns of the *Times* contain most of the charges in Dickens's indictment of chancery.."[28] The press campaign was quickly followed by parliamentary action. When the new session of Parliament opened in February the program of legislation included a reference to "serious attention" to the administration of justice, and in March the new prime minister, Russell, proposed a measure of reform of the Court of Chancery. Neither this nor another bill introduced during the summer went far enough to satisfy the *Times,* and the public controversy continued. By this time *Bleak House* was taking shape in Dickens's mind. Butt concludes, "Thus Dickens's indictment of chancery was more than merely topical. It followed in almost every respect the charges already levelled in the columns of the *Times.* In both we read of houses in chancery and wards in chancery, of dilatory and costly procedure, of wasted lives, and of legal obstructionists."[29] Dickens's art as a novelist has a concreteness, a quality that in another context Henry James described as "solidity of specification," that penetrates our feelings more sharply than the broad generalizations of a journalist. But it has to be added that the long campaign in the *Times* had moments that were as telling as any in the novel—as when a barrister reported that a case could not be brought to a conclusion until twenty thousand sheets of legal documents had been examined. It is a moment that brings us very close to the court that is attended by Miss Flite and that blights the youth and hopes of Richard Carstone, as well as to that other, parodic court presided over by Krook.

Jo the crossing-sweeper provides an occasion for Dickens not merely to exercise his skill in the pathetic but to render the plight of many homeless children in mid-nineteenth-century London. It is, however, characteristic of Dickens's imagination and moral passion that they were ignited by specific cases that came to his attention rather than by general problems. The prototype of Jo was almost certainly George Ruby, a boy of about fourteen who was called as a witness at the Guildhall on 8 January 1850. Four days later the *Examiner* published an article, which may well have been written by Dickens himself, in which the following cross-examination of George Ruby is quoted:

He looked quite astonished upon taking hold of the book [i.e., the Bible].
ALDERMAN HUMPHREY: Well, do you know what you are about. Do you
   know what an oath is?
BOY: No.
ALDERMAN HUMPHREY: Do you know what a Testament is?
BOY: No.
ALDERMAN HUMPHREY: Do you ever say your prayers?
BOY: No, never.
ALDERMAN HUMPHREY: Do you know what prayers are?
BOY: No.
ALDERMAN HUMPHREY: Do you know what the Devil is?
BOY: No. I've heard of the Devil, but I don't know him.
ALDERMAN HUMPHREY: What do you know my poor fellow?
BOY: I knows how to sweep a crossing.
ALDERMAN HUMPHREY: And that's all?
BOY: That's all. I sweeps the crossing.

Dickens's account of the inquest on "Nemo" (Captain Hawdon) in
chapter 11 includes a passage that is very close to the above (199).[30]

The case of George Ruby received additional publicity in the same
month when it was referred to in *The Household Narrative,* the
monthly supplement to *Household Words.* And some nineteen months
later, at just about the time Dickens was thinking deeply about his new
novel, he published in *Household Words* a review of a book by Mary
Carpenter, a well-known philanthropist, titled *Reformatory Schools.*
The reviewer, James Hannay, quoted from the book a version of
George Ruby's court appearance: " 'A boy of fourteen' meets the eye,
who recently told the alderman on the bench that he did not know
'what an oath is, what the Testament is, what prayers are, what God is,
what the devil is. *I sweeps the crossing,*' he added—summing up his
position, moral and social, in the universe, in that one sentence" (30
August 1851). Dickens, who scrutinized everything that appeared in
his magazine, would thus have had his memory refreshed concerning
the poignant case of the young crossing-sweeper.

As Mary Carpenter's book demonstrated in detail, George Ruby
was not an isolated figure: the problem of juvenile vagrancy was a
large one. It was also highly topical and, as Trevor Blount says, "very

much a matter of public concern"[31] in the period when *Bleak House* was being written. A select committee of the House of Commons on criminal and destitute juveniles had issued its report on 24 June 1852, shortly after work on the novel was begun; and in the following year Carpenter published another book, *Juvenile Delinquents; Their Condition and Treatment.* Dickens's Jo contributed to focusing public attention on this problem: the character was enormously popular with readers and according to one reviewer had "already become a proverb"[32] by the time the novel appeared in volume form.

Jo's occupation may puzzle a modern reader, but it vividly evokes the contemporary urban scene. Henry Mayhew's voluminous and fascinating survey of urban workers, *London Labour and the London Poor* (1851), estimated that the "quantity of dung produced by the 7,300,000 horses which traverse the London streets" would in one year amount to "36,662 tons of horse-dung annually dropped in the streets of London." Crossing the street could therefore have been an unpleasant and even a difficult business, especially for a daintily shod lady or gentleman; and crossing-sweepers such as Jo kept crossings swept clean and lived off the pennies and halfpence given them for their services.

Jo lives in the slum that Dickens calls Tom-All-Alone's, whose importance in the novel is suggested by its appearance in some of the titles that Dickens considered and eventually rejected. It was modeled on an actual London slum, that of St. Giles, which, as Blount has shown, was brought to the attention of middle-class Londoners by an unusual letter that appeared in the *Times* on 5 July 1849 under the title "A Sanitary Remonstrance." This semiliterate but graphic document was signed by fifty-four slum dwellers, who described the conditions in which they and their families lived: "muck . . . no priviz [privies], no dust bins, no drains, no water-splies. . . . We all of us suffer, and numbers are ill." Four days later the *Times*, which Dickens is known to have read regularly, published an article describing the experiences of an investigator who, prompted by the letter, had gone to see for himself the notorious slum and had found there "an endless repetition of filth and degradation" in the heart of a prosperous city.[33]

In *Bleak House* the lower-middle-class Snagsby is taken by Bucket on a tour of Tom-All-Alone's in chapter 22; but between the revelations in the *Times* and the writing of the novel Dickens himself had experienced a similar tour in similar company. In a *Household Words* article, "On Duty with Inspector Field," on 14 June 1851 he recounted a visit to the "rookery" or slum of St. Giles and wrote: "How many [inhabitants of London], who amidst this compound of sickening smells, these heaps of filth, these tumbling houses, with all their vile contents, animate and inanimate, slimily overflowing into the black road, would believe that they breathe *this* air?" In the novel the idea of infection spreading from the slums to the respectable parts of the city is central; in this article, written months before work on *Bleak House* began, it is already lightly touched on. Public health was much in Dickens's mind in the summer of 1851. On 10 May, just after the opening of the Great Exhibition, he said in a speech to the Metropolitan Sanitary Association that "no one can estimate the amount of mischief which is grown in dirt; . . . no one can say, here it stops, or there it stops, either in its physical or its moral results, when both begin in the cradle and are not at rest in the obscene grave"—another anticipation of *Bleak House*. He added that sanitary reform "must precede all other social remedies, and even Education and Religion can do nothing where they are most needed, until the way is paved for in their ministrations by Cleanliness and Decency." His passionate convictions about the importance of sanitary reform should be seen in the context both of the prevailing conditions of the day—including London streets offensive to the eye and the nose and a Thames heavily polluted—and of what a modern critic has referred to as "Dickens's worship [in his private life] of order and cleanliness"[34]—this last perhaps a deeply ingrained response to the circumstances of his early years and especially the rat-infested warehouse in which he had traumatically worked.

Again, the whole subject was a topical one. Between 1849 and 1852 a series of reports on sanitary conditions in various towns had appeared, and in 1852 the medical superintending inspector of the Board of Health, Dr. John Sutherland, had published his *Reports on the Sanitary Condition of the Epidemic Districts of the Metropolis, with Special Reference to the Threatened Visitation of Epidemic Cholera.* As Sutherland's title suggests, the problem of unspeakably bad housing conditions in the slums was linked with the problem of disease. The connection is fully exploited in Dickens's novel, where the "fever" is both a contemporary fact and a powerful symbol.

Epidemics of serious infectious diseases were commonplace in nineteenth-century England. There had been an outbreak of cholera during Dickens's youth, in 1831–2, and it had reappeared in 1848–9. There were many medical discussions of its causes, such as John Snow's pamphlet "On the Mode of Communication of Cholera" (1849) and William Budd's pamphlet "Malignant Cholera: Its Mode of Propagation and its Prevention" in the same year; there was also much publicity at a more popular level, such as a cartoon "A Court for King Cholera" that appeared in *Punch* in 1852. Scarlet fever epidemics occurred in 1840, 1844, and 1848 and continued at intervals for the rest of the century. Diphtheria was rife not only in England but in Europe and North America. Typhoid outbreaks, like other diseases of this kind, were no respecters of rank, and the prince consort died of this cause in 1861. In *Bleak House* it is smallpox that lays low both Charley and Esther. Contemporary attempts to control this disease through vaccination made it a topical issue. A serious epidemic in 1837–40 had produced a Vaccination Act (1840), which was followed by the Vaccination Extension Act of 1853, making vaccination within four months of birth compulsory. During Dickens's lifetime medical understanding of some of these diseases was very incomplete, and for the purposes of registering deaths the omnibus term *fever* was used.[35]

Overcrowding, filth, disease, and infection are also related in the novel to another contemporary issue: the city graveyards. Here again Trevor Blount's researches have demonstrated the closeness of the fictional to the actual world. In chapter 11 Dickens describes the burial of Nemo in "a hemmed-in churchyard, pestiferous and obscene, whence malignant diseases are communicated to the bodies of our dear brothers and sisters who have not departed" (202). The passage continues in circumstantial detail:

With houses looking on, on every side, save where a reeking little tunnel of a court gives access to the iron gate—with every villainy of life in action close on death, and every poisonous element of death in action close on life—here, they lower our dear brother down a foot or two: here, sow him in corruption, to be raised in corruption: an avenging ghost at many a sick-bedside: a shameful testimony to future ages, how civilization and barbarism walked this boastful island together.

Readers of this passage would have been aware that, as Blount says, "the administrative reform of intramural burial-grounds in the London Metropolitan area was pressing and topical."[36]

A few years earlier the *Times* (5 March 1845) had published a horrifying account of the conditions at Spa Fields Burial Ground: there, corpses were crammed into shallow graves and "The stench arising from decomposed human bodies was . . . insufferable," as the avarice of sextons and gravediggers led them to accept bodies for burial long after the available space was filled. As Jo tells Lady Dedlock, "They put him [Nemo] wery nigh the top. They was obliged to stamp upon it to git it in. I could unkiver it for you with my broom, if the gate was open" (278). G. A. Walker's *Burial-Ground Incendiarism* (1846) had given further publicity to the problem, and Dickens had published an article, "Heathen and Christian Burial," in *Household Words* (6 April 1850), written jointly by his subeditor W. H. Wills and his father-in-law George Hogarth, that referred to the abominable custom of "consigning mortal remains to closely-packed burial-grounds in crowded cities; covering—scarcely interring them . . . —while the exhalations of putrefaction always vitiate the air." In such passages we are, as so often, very close to the ideas and even the language of the novel. Agitation on the part of Walker and others led to the passing of the Metropolitan Interments Act of 1850, but, as usual, practical reforms did not immediately follow legislative action.

Jo is not the only character in *Bleak House* with strongly topical elements, and not the only one who may have had a real-life prototype. Dickens's instinct was to personalize problems and issues: to present large, general questions in terms of highly specific, vividly individualized personalities who were at the same time allegedly representative. The comic and satiric figure of Mrs. Jellyby, who specializes in "telescopic philanthropy"(charitable efforts directed at distant objects, while those much nearer home are overlooked), is an excellent example, according to House, of "the strength and the weakness of Dickens's use of fiction as a medium of social criticism: [the episode] is prodigiously strong in personalities, but weak in arguments." House suggests that Dickens's readers would have recognized an allusion to the African Civilization Society and Niger Association, which, about ten years before the novel appeared, had organized under royal patronage an expedition to West Africa. One of its objects was "to establish a model farm there as a centre of beneficent Christian civilization"; but a large number of the colonists died of fever, and the experiment was soon abandoned.[37]

Onto this fairly recent event Dickens may have grafted a personality whom he had come to know even more recently. On 26 February 1850 he met Mrs. Caroline Chisholm, whom the *Dictionary of National Biography* describes as "the emigrant's friend" and of whom it says that "her energy knew no limit." Mrs. Chisholm had been in Australia from 1838 to 1846, where she had established a Female Immigrants' Home in Sydney. Back in England, she worked indefatigably to establish a society to make loans to families wishing to emigrate. She also wrote widely about her scheme (we recall Mrs. Jellyby's immense correspondence concerning Borrioboola-Gha): in 1850 she published her *ABC of Colonization,* and in the same year, in the very first number of Dickens's magazine *Household Words* (30 March), she coauthored with him an article titled "A Bundle of Emigrants' Letters." Mrs. Chisholm seems to have been too busy to give much time to her children or her home, and after Dickens visited her, he wrote to a friend (3 April 1850), "I dream of Mrs. Chisholm and her housekeeping. The dirty faces of her children are my continual companions." It seems likely that memories of the abortive and ill-advised African Civilization Society and Niger Association merged with his more recent observation of Mrs. Chisholm's home conditions to produce Mrs. Jellyby. If so, the portrait was certainly unfair to Mrs. Chisholm; for while Mrs. Jellyby knows nothing of Africa, her real-life counterpart had a firsthand knowledge of the problems of Australian settlers. But exaggeration, even at the price of unfairness to individuals, was, as his contemporaries were quick to recognize, the essence of Dickens's method. A further detail confirming this identification is that Mrs. Jellyby's eldest daughter, who may well have been named after her mother in accordance with custom, shares Mrs. Chisholm's name, Caroline. After the failure of the African scheme, Mrs. Jellyby turns her attention to another topical issue that Dickens was quick to satirize: the rights of women.

In August 1848 in the *Examiner* Dickens had reviewed an account of the ill-fated 1841 expedition to the Niger, and he wrote there that "the work at home must be completed thoroughly, or there is no hope abroad." Mrs. Jellyby exemplifies the failure to act on this belief, and she is not the only character in the novel to do so. Mrs. Pardiggle is a formidable doer of good works, but her own children are miserable, and when she visits the wretched brickmaker's family, she brings neither sympathy nor comfort.

Mrs. Pardiggle also embodies a reference to the religious controversies of the day. During the previous twenty years many members of the Church of England had become dismayed by the growing influence of the Oxford Movement, also known as the Tractarian Movement, led from 1841 by distinguished Oxford professor Edward Pusey. This High Church movement seemed to many to bring the English church disturbingly closer to Rome in its doctrines and practices; and when the Roman Catholic hierarchy was established in England, Dickens himself described it in a letter (22 August 1851) as an "intolerable enormity." Mrs. Pardiggle, whose children are (in accordance with Anglo-Catholic fashion) named after saints and heroes of the early church, is a representative of the Puseyites; and there is another reference to the same topic in chapter 8, where Mr. Jarndyce is asked to contribute to a fund "to establish in a picturesque building . . . the Sisterhood of Mediaeval Marys" (150). Pusey had helped to establish the first Anglican sisterhood in 1845, so this is again an allusion to recent history.

A very different figure who also belongs to the contemporary scene is Inspector Bucket. One of England's achievements in the second quarter of the nineteenth century was the creation for the first time of an efficient police force. The Metropolitan Police had been established in 1829, and "by 1856, the whole country was policed by full-time paid forces on the new model."[38] The detective section of the force was established in 1842, and "though it remained very small in numbers throughout this period it soon had earned a record of creditable achievement. By the 1850s, the popular prestige and mystique of the Detective had become established."[39]

Bucket is often regarded as the first detective in English fiction. He seems to have been based on Inspector Charles Field, about whom Dickens had written in several *Household Words* articles in 1850. (These pieces were later collected in Dickens's volume of sketches titled *Reprinted Pieces*.) In "The Detective Police" Field is described as "a middle-aged man of a portly presence, with a large, moist, knowing eye, a husky voice, and a habit of emphasising his conversation by the aid of a corpulent fore-finger, which is constantly is juxtaposition with his eyes or nose" (27 July 1850). Compare this with the description of Bucket on his first appearance as "a stoutly built, steady-looking, sharp-eyed man in black, of about the middle-age" (361) and the frequent references thereafter to his use of his forefinger. Just as Snagsby accompanies Bucket on a visit to Tom-All-Alone's, Dickens accompanied Field on a tour of the criminal quarters of London. Dickens's experiences are recounted in another essay, "On Duty with Inspector Field," in which the detective's professional skill, confidence, and authority bear a strong resemblance to the characteristics of Bucket: "Every thief here cowers before him, like a schoolboy before his schoolmaster. All watch him, all answer when addressed, all laugh at his jokes, all seek to propitiate him" (14 June 1851).

Dickens's view of the detective is, as Collins says, dramatic and romantic; but he also has a respect and even a fellow-feeling for a notable member of this new profession who is, like himself, a self-made man, a dealer in secrets, and an unraveler of mysteries. In another *Household Words* article of 13 July 1850, "The Modern Science of Thief-taking," he had referred to one of the functions of the detective as being "to clear up family mysteries, the identification of which demands the utmost delicacy and tact." This is of course precisely Bucket's role in *Bleak House,* and the character provides a neat example of Dickens's method of calling attention to a significant new development in contemporary society and at the same time drawing on his knowledge of an individual whose character and role had seized his imagination.

Dickens was fascinated by crime in all its aspects, by criminals as well as detectives. The sinister figure of Hortense, lady's maid to Lady Dedlock and later the murderer of Tulkinghorn, would have been quickly recognized by many of his readers as based on a protagonist in a celebrated criminal case that was only three years old, still fresh in the memories of most readers of 1852–53. On 13 November 1849 about thirty thousand people had witnessed the execution in London of Mr. and Mrs. George Manning, who had been convicted of brutally murdering their lodger. (Hangings were held in public until near the end of Dickens's lifetime.) Dickens was in the crowd, and its behavior angered and revolted him so much that he wrote two letters to the *Times,* the first on the very day of the execution. These letters precipitated a considerable controversy on the subject of public executions, and Dickens soon found himself, as he put it, "in the midst of . . . a roaring sea of correspondence" on this subject. The letters do not touch on the rights and wrongs of capital punishment but stress that executions should take place inside prisons rather than being public spectacles.

The execution was sensationalized partly because it was said to be the first time in 150 years that a husband and wife had been hanged together. Of the two, the wife seems to have been the more remarkable personality. As Collins says, "Maria Manning had captured the public imagination. She was a Belgian, of intrepid and passionate temperament. During the trial she kept interrupting the Judge with cries of 'There is no law nor justice to be got here! Base and degraded England!' In prison she behaved furiously and violently, cursing all the officers, and making a remarkably bold attempt to commit suicide."[40] In *Bleak House* Hortense, a Frenchwoman, shares Mrs. Manning's "intrepid and passionate temperament," and it seems highly probable that the latter had captured the imagination of Dickens as well as that of the public at large.

In the same year as the trial and execution of the Mannings, a different kind of sensation was caused by the Tooting baby-farm scandal. At Tooting in south London a man called Drouet kept fourteen hundred pauper children in a baby-farm in conditions of appalling overcrowding and neglect. In 1848, cholera broke out there, and many of the young children died. Disclosures at the inquests made the affair public, and there was an outcry. Drouet was later tried for manslaughter, but, as House points out, part of the blame also belonged to "the various London Boards of Guardians who sent their children to the place, and to the central Poor Law authority which allowed it to continue."[41] At the beginning of 1849 Dickens wrote two articles for the *Examiner* attacking the system that had allowed such a tragedy to take place, declaring that the epidemic had broken out "in Mr Drouet's farm for children, because it was brutally conducted, vilely kept, preposterously inspected, dishonestly defended, a disgrace to a Christian community, and a stain upon a civilized land" (January 1849).

In *Bleak House* the pathetic figure of Guster, the Snagsbys' overworked servant girl, is the occasion for several references to the Tooting scandal. On her first appearance Guster is described as "a lean young woman from a workhouse; . . . who, although she was farmed or contracted for during her growing time, by an amiable benefactor of his species resident at Tooting, and cannot fail to have been developed under the most favourable circumstances, 'has fits'—which the parish can't account for" (180). Dickens adds that Guster, "really aged three or four and twenty, but looking a round ten years older," lives in constant terror of being sent back to "her patron saint": presumably a reference to the ill-famed Drouet, whose name is never actually mentioned in the novel. Few who read the novel on its first appearance, however, would have had difficulty in supplying it.

Not all the instances of topicality discussed in this chapter are of equal importance. Whereas Chancery and slum conditions are obviously central issues, allusions such as those to the Mannings' execution and to the Tooting baby-farm are much more marginal. All, however, bear out the suggestion made earlier that Dickens did not initiate campaigns for reform but lent his literary powers and his great personal popularity to the support of causes that were already before the public and in some instances before Parliament or the courts. Collectively, these allusions must have given contemporary readers a distinct sense of reading a novel whose action was set in their own day; but, as indicated earlier, this impression is contradicted by Dickens's deliberate distancing of the action at the end of the novel. The inconsistency cannot readily be resolved except by arguing that presumably to Dickens such considerations were not of great importance. The final distancing serves the immediate purpose of reassuring the reader about the afterlives of the principal characters, but it does not work retroactively to convince us that the main action takes place at any time far from the date of composition and publication. Butt concludes his discussion of the topicality of *Bleak House* by affirming "the strong flavour of contemporaneity in the action and in the characters": "*Bleak House* began as a tract for the times, and the more fully this is recognized, the more fully we shall appreciate the 'esemplastic power' which imposed upon a mass of seemingly heterogeneous material a significant and acceptable form."[42]

5

Connection: Story and Plot, Society and Class

As his extraordinary career progressed, Dickens set himself—and triumphantly solved—a daunting problem: how to give unity, coherence, and singleness of purpose to a very long novel presenting a panoramic picture of society. The structure of his early novels is mainly loose and episodic, but it is generally agreed that, from *Dombey and Son* (1846–48) onward, Dickens attempted to construct a much more carefully planned and integrated kind of fiction in which characters and events are not arbitrary or gratuitous but are intimately related to the overall purpose. In chapter 1 I have shown evidence for this in the "working notes" that Dickens made to assist his planning of the novel, and evidence of another kind may be found within the text of the novel itself. On its very early pages, for instance, are hints (not necessarily obvious on a first reading) of what is to come much later.

These hints are most obviously manifested on the level of plot— the element that stresses causality and the interrelatedness of happenings, the way in which one event is connected with another even though they may be widely separated in time and place and circumstances. *Plot* is an ambiguous term and can refer to ordinary human planning of a secretive kind as well as to the specialized professional planning of a novelist. Dickens seems to have been aware of this ambiguity and to have seen himself as not only a craftsman constructing plots (as other craftsmen construct chairs and tables) but, within the "world" of the novel, as one who fulfils the functions of God or Providence in the real world. When the lawyer Mr. Kenge tells Esther that her life is to take a wholly unexpected change of direction as a result of Mr. Jarndyce's decision to assume responsibility for her education, he says that this will enable her "to discharge her duty in that station of life unto which it has pleased—shall we say Providence?—to call her" (69). The "plot" of Esther's life at this point seems as if it were being made by Jarndyce, but of course the reader is well aware that he is only a fiction created by Dickens, the supreme plot-maker.

More than a little surprising, therefore, is the complaint of one early reviewer of *Bleak House,* the well-known critic George Brimley, about its "absolute want of construction," adding that "Mr Dickens discards plot."[43] As this reminds us, a classic novel such as *Bleak House* was in its time so completely "modern" and original as to baffle even experienced readers. For the modern reader there is surely no shortage of plot, nor of evidence of Dickens's skill and farsightedness in linking widely separated details. One of the main concerns of the novel is the inescapability of the past and the emergence of what has been hidden into the light of day. Naturally enough, therefore, one of its key words is *secret,* and a careful reading of the text registers its appearances on the early pages of the text. In the second chapter we learn of the 'secrets . . . shut up in the breast of Mr Tulkinghorn' (58), and the word is quickly taken up by Esther when she begins her narrative in the following chapter: as a child she tells her doll "every one of my secrets" (62), but she is also surrounded by mysteries to which she does not know the answer, especially concerning her parentage. (When the Chancery judge makes an inquiry about her parentage, the answer is "whispered" (p. 79) to him by Kenge and not heard by Esther.)

The narrative method ensures that the reader, like Esther and most other characters, is ignorant of these secrets, since neither the third-person narrator nor Esther herself offers an explanation of the numerous mysteries that confront the reader in the early part of the book. We are bound to wonder, for instance: Who are Esther's parents? Who is the mysteriously named Nemo (Latin for *nobody*)? Why does Lady Dedlock react so dramatically to a glimpse of a handwritten document? And why does Guppy find himself intrigued by a portrait hanging in the Dedlock mansion? These are only a few of the secrets held by the novelist; during the course of reading the novel, not only does the reader come to know them all, but all the secrets given as examples here turn out to be related or connected. For as we shall see, *connection*—which is in one sense the opposite of *secret* (as implying revelation and understanding)—is another key word of this novel.

Dickens's placing of references to these secrets and the often gradual process of their unfolding are additional evidence of his detailed planning. Early in the novel, for instance, in chapter 7, Guppy, seeing a picture of Lady Dedlock, is at a loss to understand why it should seem familiar to him even though he has never seen it before, nor Lady Dedlock herself. Seventeen chapters later, meeting Esther, he is again puzzled: "I thought I had seen you somewhere" (397). These two widely separate passages, relatively inconspicuous though they are, are related to each other and furnish a clue to the vital question of Esther's parentage.

There are many other such hints to be picked up by a perceptive reader (though perhaps only on a second reading). Another reference to the portrait of Lady Dedlock at Chesney Wold, the country house in Lincolnshire, describes the sunshine as throwing "a broad bend-sinister of light that strikes down crookedly into the hearth, and seems to rend [the portrait]" (204). This is not only a foreshadowing of Lady Dedlock's ultimate fate (in the violent verb *rend*): if *bend-sinister* is taken not merely as a fanciful descriptive term but is given due weight, it offers another hint of the proud aristocratic lady's murky past (since bend sinister in heraldry is a symbol of bastardy). A few pages later Mrs. Rouncewell, the housekeeper, remarks that it is "almost a pity . . . that my Lady has no family. If she had had a daughter now, a grown young lady, to interest her . . ." (208)—an apparently trivial remark by a minor character, easily overlooked, but in fact a pointer to the existence of a living daughter who at this stage is equally unknown to Mrs. Rouncewell, Lady Dedlock, and the reader. Actually the first hint of this kind comes right at the beginning of the novel, when Lady Dedlock makes her first appearance: "My Lady Dedlock (who is childless) . . ." (56). The parentheses play down any significance the detail might otherwise seem to have; it is, however, crucial and also deceptive (*childless* here meaning "believing that she has no living child" or "supposed to have no child" rather than "having no child").

Again, when Esther sees Lady Dedlock in church in chapter 18, her strong but incomprehensible emotions hint at a significance not fully explained for some time. A hint on a different subject is given, unconsciously, by George Rouncewell when he remarks that at his shooting gallery he has "had French women come, before now, and show themselves dabs [experts] at pistol-shooting" (397), which once more seems to be a superfluous detail but with hindsight can be interpreted as a premonitory hint on the narrator's part of the identity of Tulkinghorn's murderer later in the novel. George's identity is similarly hinted at in a reference to Mrs. Rouncewell's "two sons, of whom the younger ran wild, and went for a soldier, and never came back" (134), while the same page contains a foreshadowing of Sir Leicester Dedlock's subsequent stroke ("if he were very ill . . ."). Finally, to complete this by no means exhaustive list of hints and foreshadowings, the references to the churchyard in which Nemo is buried ("a hemmed-in churchyard, pestiferous and obscene, whence malignant diseases are communicated to the bodies of our dear brothers and sisters who have not yet departed," 202) look forward to the infection carried by Jo and caught by Esther and Charley much later in the story.

If there are secrets and mysteries, there are also solvers or would-be solvers of secrets and mysteries. *Bleak House* offers, in Bucket, the first substantial portrayal of a detective in English fiction, but there are also many amateur detectives here who, teased and fascinated by the puzzles they encounter, seek solutions. In their quite different ways, and with varying degrees of success, both Tulkinghorn and Guppy seek to unravel the mystery of Lady Dedlock's past. At a minor level, Hortense and Mrs. Snagsby also put themselves on the track of mysteries; Mrs. Snagsby, with her quite-unfounded suspicion that her husband is the father of Jo, is of course a hopelessly incompetent detective. Guppy and Jobling are confronted by the mystery of what has happened to Krook as they behave like spies or conspirators on his premises.

All this suggests that the plotting of *Bleak House* is brilliantly contrived. Though not in itself one of Dickens's most complex plots (and we may be grateful for this, for one or two of them, such as *Little Dorrit,* are so complex as to be baffling), its details are handled with masterly skill and often with great subtlety. It will not do, however, to imply that the plot is simply an ingenious mechanical contrivance or an elaborate framework for the other elements of the novel. It also embodies an important aspect of Dickens's thinking about the nature of human experience; the workings of the plot are a reflection of the way in which life itself confronts us. To understand this better it will be helpful to look for a moment at Dickens's use of coincidence.

Coincidences—those jokes played upon us by chance in apparent defiance of the laws of probability—are part of everyone's experience. It ought not, therefore, to be a matter for complaint if a novelist's created world also contains them, though we do in fact seem to set higher standards of probability for fiction. The trouble (if it is a trouble) with Dickens's coincidences, as with those of other Victorian novelists, is that they are often decisive in affecting the major issues of life in the novels and are not merely minor curiosities. Consider for a moment some of the coincidences in the plotting of *Bleak House.* Jarndyce, who becomes Esther's guardian, is a friend of Boythorn, whose estate happens to adjoin that of Sir Leicester Dedlock—a geographical accident that enables Esther, on her visit to Boythorn's house, to come into contact with Lady Dedlock (something that could not very easily have been contrived otherwise). Moreover, Boythorn turns out to have been engaged formerly to Miss Barbary, Esther's aunt and foster mother. Again, it is remarkable that on her single short visit to the coast, when she visits Richard at Deal, Esther should happen to witness the homecoming of Allan Woodcourt (679); and that in the following chapter (46) Woodcourt should encounter Jo the crossing-sweeper and Jenny, the brickmaker's wife, both of whom have already played a role in Esther's own experience.

Any reader of the novel will be able to think of other examples, but the interesting question is whether these are instances of lazy or desperate plot-making or whether they represent a more deeply held conviction on Dickens's part. Relevant here is a comment made by his close friend and biographer, John Forster: "On the coincidences, resemblances, and surprises of life, Dickens liked especially to dwell, and few things moved his fancy so pleasantly. The world, he would say, was so much smaller than we thought it; we were all so connected by fate without knowing it; people supposed to be far apart were so constantly elbowing each other; and to-morrow bore so close a resemblance to nothing half so much as to yesterday." Some of these phrases recall the examples of coincidence cited above, and one of them echoes a key word of the novel: "we were all so connected by fate without knowing it." *Bleak House* is a novel about *connections*, those that are hidden as well as those that are apparent, and the development of the story traces the emergence of connections (for a very prominent example, that of mother and child) that have been concealed. A coincidence is a way of dramatizing or embodying in reality a connection that reminds us how little we are in control of our own destinies and how ready fate is to make patterns in our lives, patterns that suggest that we are not merely the inhabitants of a world of random and meaningless events.

The words *coincidence* and *connection* are used in two passages of the novel that are worth considering carefully. In chapter 24 Jarndyce and Esther, meeting George Rouncewell, discover that they have in common an acquaintance with the unfortunate Gridley, "the man from Shropshire" who is driven to despair and death by a Chancery suit. Esther's narrative records that "my guardian and I exchanged a word or two of surprise at the coincidence" (398). Such moments in the novel create the effect of seeing, as if through a gap in the curtain, a system or pattern that lies behind the apparent flux and confusion of everyday experience.

Earlier, and much more important, the third-person narrator opened chapter 16, "Tom-All-Alone's," with five paragraphs concerning the Dedlocks and then, before turning to Jo, asks these rhetorical questions: "What connexion can there be, between the place in Lincolnshire, the house in town, the Mercury in powder, and the whereabout of Jo the outlaw with the broom, who had that distant ray of light upon him when he swept the churchyard-step? What connexion can there have been between many people in the innumerable histories of the world, who, from opposite sides of great gulfs, have, nevertheless, been very curiously brought together!" (272). The novel itself recounts some of these "innumerable histories," and some of the characters—including such an unlikely pair as Jo and Lady Dedlock—are indeed "very curiously brought together" in the course of its action.

Dickens's preoccupation with connection or interrelatedness finds a very congenial area of operation in the image of the city. The modern city was an invention of Victorian England, and Dickens is its first great literary chronicler. In the course of a single day a city dweller encounters many people, nearly all strangers, without knowing whether some of those who are (to borrow Forster's phrase) "constantly elbowing each other" are connected to him by unknown ties in the past, or will in the future be so connected. A city crowd is thus for Dickens an emblem of human life, in its variety, in its mystery, and in the secrets it may unexpectedly yield. Although many scenes of *Bleak House* are set outside London, notably in Hertfordshire (Jarndyce's house) and Lincolnshire (the Dedlock country house), London is the scene of much of the action, and many streets and neighborhoods are precisely specified.

An important aspect of the "connection" theme is the way that experience, in defiance of expectation, cuts across the class system and brings together those who would not have imagined that their lives would ever cross. There is a specific comment on this when the dying Jo is visited by the well-to-do Jarndyce and the professional man Woodcourt, "both thinking, much, how strangely Fate has entangled this rough outcast in the web of very different lives" (703). Jo is also entangled in the web of other and even more different lives, including Lady Dedlock's, and it will be interesting to look more closely at the way Dickens's plot enacts the periodical breakdown of the rigidities of the Victorian class system. Disraeli's "two nations," the rich and the poor, in so many ways so widely separated, nevertheless come together at moments in Dickens's fictions.

One Victorian commentator said of the England of his day that it was "a paradise for the well-to-do, a purgatory for the able, and a hell for the poor."[44] In *Bleak House* Dickens portrayed the whole range of society, from the aristocratic, land-owning, and governing class, through all the numerous levels of the middle class, to the laboring poor and, at the very bottom, the destitute and the homeless. In his influential essay on Dickens, George Orwell claimed that "his real subject-matter is the London commercial bourgeoisie and their hangers-on,"[45] but this claim surely defines the range of *Bleak House* (to say nothing of the other novels) too narrowly. The "commercial bourgeoisie" is certainly a class that is very fully represented, but the world of the novel extends both higher and lower. And within a given group, such as those providing goods and services in the metropolis, there is obviously a vast difference between, say, Snagsby the law-stationer, Krook the filthy and half-crazy keeper of a junk shop, and Trooper George with his shooting gallery. The gradations of status in the servant class (as between, for instance, Mrs. Rouncewell, Hortense, and Guster) have already been noted and are very wide. Consider also the differences between the various representatives of the legal profession: Tulkinghorn enjoys greater status and affluence than Vholes.

It follows that such concepts as class, group, and category need to be approached with caution: Dickens is more interested in what makes people different from each other, and even unique, than in what they have in common. *Middle class* is a particularly inclusive label, covering a wide range of socioeconomic statuses, from that of Jarndyce and Boythorn, who are men of independent means, through the various gradations of the professional and commercial classes, to such lower-middle-class figures as Snagsby and Guppy. Nor is society static: Dickens was well aware that he lived in a time of unprecedented social mobility, and in a character such as Rouncewell the iron-master he depicts a member of a newly emerging class that achieved wealth and power in the nineteenth century, that of the industrialist; Rouncewell's humble origins (he is the son of a servant) are no obstacle to success in the career he has so energetically adopted.

Dickens is also interested in those who cannot be easily placed in relation to the existing social order. As a writer and self-made man who rose from early poverty to wealth, fame, and the life-style of a gentleman, he had every reason to be sensitive to those whose status was uncertain or anomalous. Bucket, for instance, is a member of a brand-new profession, a detective, and while he lacks the polished manners of a professional man such as Tulkinghorn, he has the self-confidence that comes from knowledge of his own skill and power. Chadband is a preacher "of no particular denomination": that is, he does not belong to the established church, which would place him readily on the social scale, but is the popular leader of a lower-class nonconformist congregation. Turveydrop, modeling himself on the prince regent, has a social manner that suggests a class considerably above his actual status. Another survivor from an earlier period, Skimpole, defines his own role: when Sir Leicester asks him whether he is an artist, Skimpole replies in the negative and claims to be "A perfectly idle man. A mere amateur" (659). As Dickens's comment implies ("Sir Leicester seemed to approve of this . . ."), Skimpole is claiming a socioeconomic status that renders it unnecessary for him to pursue any profession seriously; the reader is in a position to know that his amateurism is mere trifling and that his financial affairs are very precarious, though his indifference to the claims of his creditors enables him to enjoy such upper-class luxuries as hothouse peaches.

W. J. Harvey has suggested that "the fragmented individual" and "the fragmented society" are important themes of this novel: characters are isolated by the social system, with the result that they are unaware of the realities of other lives physically close to their own. Referring to the episode in which the unworldly but humane Snagsby accompanies Inspector Bucket on a tour of the slum of Tom-All-Alone's (as Dickens himself had accompanied Inspector Field, the prototype of Bucket, on visits to London slums), Harvey asks: "What can the Boodles know of Jo or Jenny when Snagsby, who lives not far away, can be appalled by the unfamiliar hell of Tom-All-Alone's?"[46] At the same time Dickens does show that members of different groups and classes can become aware of the plight of their fellowmen, sometimes by being brought dramatically face to face with them (as various middle-class characters, and even the aristocratic Lady Dedlock, are made aware of Jo the crossing-sweeper). He shows this partly by contrivances of the plot but also by an elaborate system of parallels or echoes that relate one character and situation to another and thus bring together what appear to be separate elements of the novel in a way that cuts across the divisions of class.

Allusion has already been made to some of the moments when the narrative contrives encounters between representatives of very different social levels, as when (for instance) Esther, Mrs. Pardiggle, and Lady Dedlock all visit the brickmaker's wife in her wretched home, when Snagsby visits the slum that is Jo's unsavory dwelling, and when Jo and Lady Dedlock visit the churchyard together. Another kind of linking is effected by the fever (presumably smallpox) that crosses the boundaries of class and, originating in the appalling sanitary conditions of the slum, invades the middle-class world of Bleak House and, literally, leaves its mark upon Esther. The disease is both a contemporary medical fact and a symbol, like the London fog in the opening chapter, and its spread graphically illustrates Dickens's themes of connection and of the way in which the well-being of one section of society is bound up with that of all the others. Not far from Dickens's mind seems to be St. Paul's declaration (Eph. 4.25) that we are all "members one of another."

Finally, one of the most fascinating features of *Bleak House* is that apparently unrelated characters turn out on reflection to be variations on the same theme and linked by fundamental resemblances. Turveydrop and Mrs. Jellyby never meet, but they both exemplify an absorption in self-centered preoccupations that renders them indifferent to their real duties and obligations and that leads them to exploit others; Turveydrop and Sir Leicester Dedlock belong to very different social spheres, but both represent an archaic, parasitical clinging to forms of behavior and thought that have no place in the contemporary world (and Turveydrop's lament concerning the "levelling age" [246] actually echoes the baronet's snobbish objections to socially mobile and politically radical men such as the iron-master). Turveydrop and Skimpole also have much in common; with a bold imaginative stroke Dickens even draws a parallel between Krook and the Lord Chancellor, not only bestowing the latter's title as a nickname upon the former but hinting at a symbolic parallel between the shop, with its piles of accumulated rubbish, and the unreformed legal system. These are only a few of the links between different parts of the novel; a close reading will suggest many others, and all serve to reinforce the importance of connection as an overarching theme of the novel.

6

Narrative Method

One of the crucial decisions a novelist must make before writing a single word concerns narrative point of view. As one critic has said, "The choice of a point of view in the writing of fiction is at least as crucial as the choice of a verse form in the composing of a poem."[47] We have only to consider how profoundly different a book *Jane Eyre*, for instance, would be if the story were told by an anonymous third-person narrator rather than by the heroine, or how the effect of *Tess of the D'Urbervilles* would be changed by having the heroine tell her own story, to appreciate the importance of this element.

Before *Bleak House*, most of Dickens's novels had employed what is usually referred to as the "omniscient narrator" (though in his first novel, *Pickwick Papers*, he interpolated a number of short first-person narratives). The major exception is the novel that immediately preceded *Bleak House: David Copperfield*, serialized in 1849–50, is presented as the autobiography of the eponymous hero. (Dickens had in fact begun an autobiography, of which no more than a small portion was written, not long before beginning *Copperfield;* the success of Charlotte Brontë's *Jane Eyre* may also have led to his attempting a work in this form.)

Narrative Method

Bleak House is, however, different from any of the novels that preceded it. Indeed, it is unique in Dickens's work and is, by any standard, remarkably innovative. Its double narrative employs two irregularly alternating narrators: the third-person narrator who begins the story in the first two chapters, and the first-person narrator who takes it up in the third chapter and thereafter is responsible for almost exactly half the narrative. The first narrator is anonymous, objective, and presumably masculine and stands outside the action; the second is named (Esther Summerson, later Esther Woodcourt), subjective, feminine, and a major character in the story. A few of the monthly installments are narrated wholly by one or the other, but most are divided between the two narrators; the reader of *Bleak House* is thus exposed to two contrasting voices. By the end, the impersonal narrator has given us thirty-four chapters and Esther thirty-three.

Dickens must have realized at the outset that he would need to differentiate sharply between these two voices in order to avoid confusing the reader, and he did so in several ways. Most obviously, perhaps, is the use of a different verb tense for each. Whereas Esther's narrative is retrospective (she is writing her story, which is a kind of autobiography, seven years after the conclusion of the action) and uses the past tense normal for such narratives, the third-person narrator uses the present tense. Nor is this the only stylistic contrast. Her language is for the most part simple and at times even banal, and her tone informal and confidential; the other narrative by contrast is rhetorical, linguistically experimental, and dramatic. This contrast is obvious from a glance at the openings of the first and third chapters. Chapter 1 begins with a one-word sentence ("London."), soon follows it with another verbless sentence ("Implacable November weather."), and proceeds to use picturesque imagery and a richly exotic vocabulary. ("Megalosaurus" and "elephantine" are both used in the opening paragraph, for instance.) Esther's narrative, on the other hand, begins with the first-person pronoun and uses the language of everyday speech in a manner that seems artless and even naïve. Sentence structures are of a kind that reflects the conversation or letter-writing of a young girl. ("I had never heard my mama spoken of. I had never heard of my papa

either, but I felt more interested about my mama.") Dickens's manuscript shows that this chapter opening gave him a good deal of trouble,
and there are many revisions on the first page or two: evidently he
considered it essential to establish the tone of Esther's discourse—and
contrast it with that of the other narrative—at the outset.

Language and style apart, there are further differences between the
two narratives. Esther's, for instance, is more consistently serious; most
of the comedy in this novel (and there is a good deal) is found in the
more imaginative and highly colored third-person narrative. Again, it is
impossible for Esther to enjoy the freedom and mobility of the other
narrator: as a young woman living in a middle-class family, her move-
ments are strictly circumscribed, and though she travels from Mr.
Jarndyce's house in Hertfordshire to London (not far to the south), to
Mr. Boythorn's house in Lincolnshire (a considerably greater distance
to the north), and even as far as the coast (when she visits Richard
Carstone at Deal in Kent), she cannot experience the variety of scenes or
encounter the vast range of characters that the other narrator is able to
present to the reader.

At the same time there is a substantial overlap between the two
narratives. They proceed more or less concurrently, and a number of
people and places are referred to by both narrators. The reader does
not, however, simply see the same thing twice over but is endowed
with a kind of double vision. This demands, as Jeremy Hawthorn has
said, an agility and flexibility of response:

> The double narrative . . . causes [the reader] continually to "reset"
> his or her attitude to what is depicted. We can say that this helps to
> convey the complexity of the world and of life; we are continually
> reminded that things look differently from different viewpoints, and
> so we cannot comfortably relax into "seeing" the world through
> one fixed and reliable perspective; as we shift from the anonymous
> narrator to Esther, and back again, we keep being faced with prob-
> lems of reconciling their viewpoints and values, and this makes the
> reader an active searcher after meaning rather than merely passive
> recipient of an authorial or narrative "truth. . . ."
>   It is not, for example, that what the anonymous narrator tells

us about Lady Dedlock is neatly complemented by what Esther tells us. There are tensions and gaps between the two accounts; we do not get a seamless and complete picture of her by joining together the alternative views of her provided by the two narrators. Much the same can be said of the portrayal of Inspector Bucket, about whom we learn rather different things from the two narrators.[48]

As Hawthorn says, the outcome of the narrative method of *Bleak House* is to undermine the notion of "omniscience" and to make the reader "morally active": we cannot simply accept the authority of a narrator who is completely in charge and to whom the "truths" of the fiction are completely accessible. Instead, we are compelled to make judgments—an appropriate activity in reading a novel that is so largely concerned with the law.

In effecting the transitions from one narrative to the other, Dickens sometimes shows their relationship to one another. Chapter 6, for instance, ends with Esther going to bed; chapter 7 opens with the words, "While Esther sleeps, and while Esther wakes, it is still wet weather down at the place in Lincolnshire" (131). As Grahame Smith has said, "It is as though the eye of the film camera moved from the intimacy of the close-up to the widest possible panorama in which the individual is not forgotten ('While Esther sleeps'), but seen to be part of an infinitely more complex world than he or she can conceive."[49] On another level, the use of Esther's name instantly marks the change of narrator, as does the shift of tense from "rang me hopefully to bed" to "sleeps" and "wakes." And at certain points one narrative echoes another. This is particularly effective when Esther mentions in passing, and without awareness of the significance of what she is saying, something that has already been expounded more fully by the other narrator.

When Esther first visits London, for instance, she refers to "the dirtiest and darkest streets that ever were seen in the world" (76) and mentions "a churchyard" and "gravestones." The filth and fog of London have already been evoked in the brilliant opening chapter: Esther is subjectively reaffirming the truth that has been stated objectively and at greater length, without realizing that she is doing so. (For, while the impersonal narrator is aware of Esther, she is unaware of any narrative but her own). As for her references to a churchyard and gravestones, they are anticipating—or, to use Dickens's favorite term, "foreshadowing"—scenes later in the novel. Again, when she visits Krook's house, Esther hears from Caddy Jellyby that there has recently been "a sudden death there, and an inquest" (250). This is no news to the reader, who had a full account of the inquest three chapters earlier from the impersonal narrator.

Some other points about the two interrelated narratives can best be made by considering each in turn. Readers may sometimes be tempted to refer to the voice of the impersonal narrator as that of Dickens, but the temptation should be resisted: the impersonal narrator is as much a creation of the author as is Esther or any other named character in the novel. *Impersonal,* in fact, is a somewhat misleading term, since this narrator is far from being cool and aloof but is on the contrary passionately engaged and assertive. For the same reason, *objective* is not altogether a happy term for the third-person narrator. Perhaps less obviously, the label *omniscient,* customarily attached to such narrators and used by some critics in connection with this novel, is less than wholly appropriate.

We can see this by looking at a particular episode, that in which Guppy and his friend discover that Krook has perished from spontaneous combustion. Dickens creates in masterly fashion an atmosphere of suspense and horror, and these qualities are enhanced by the fact that the narrator seems to share the appalled uncertainty of the characters as to what has happened. Consider the following:

> "What in the Devil's name," [Guppy] says, "is this! Look at my fingers!"
> A thick, yellow liquor defiles them, which is offensive to the touch and sight and more offensive to the smell. A stagnant, sickening oil, with some natural repulsion in it that makes them both shudder. (509)

Here the narrator describes, meticulously and with a kind of revolted sensuousness, what Guppy is referring to; but there is no attempt to *explain.* The narrator is a sharp-eyed observer—looking, as it were, over Guppy's shoulder—but in the present tense of the unfolding narrative, the narrator has no access to privileged information. A little later, when Krook's room is found to be apparently empty, the narrator shares first the puzzlement of the characters and then their horrified realization of the truth:

> Is he hanging somewhere? They look up. No. . . .
> Here is a small burnt patch of flooring; here is the tinder from a little bundle of burnt paper, but not so light as usual, seeming to be steeped in something; and here is—is it the cinder of a small charred and broken log of wood sprinkled with white ashes, or is it coal? O Horror, he *is* here! and this from which we run away, striking out the light and overturning one another into the street, is all that represents him.
> Help, help, help! come into this house for Heaven's sake! (511)

The doubt conveyed by "seeming" and the questions the narrator puts to himself; the shock of discovery ("O Horror"); and above all the brilliant stroke whereby the narrator is presented as running headlong out of the house ("*we* run away") and colliding with the characters— these constitute a narrator who is far from being omniscient but who is a kind of reporter or a skilled and highly articulate eyewitness of what passes before his fascinated gaze.

The observer's or witness's role is again played by the narrator in the account of the murder of Tulkinghorn in chapter 48:

> What's that? Who fired a gun or pistol? Where was it? . . .
> Has Mr Tulkinghorn been disturbed? . . . (719–20)

This narrative stance contributes to the novel's emphasis on secrets: where an omniscient narrator would clarify and elucidate, Dickens's narrator shares with the reader his own suspicions and uncertainties. Characteristically, the discovery of Tulkinghorn's death is narrated obliquely. Instead of being *told* what has happened the reader is *shown* what is taking place:

> . . . a little after the coming of the day, come people to clean the
> rooms. And . . . the foremost of them goes wild; for, looking up at
> [the Roman's] outstretched hand, and looking down at what is
> below it, that person shrieks and flies. The others, looking in as the
> first one looked, shriek and fly too, and there is an alarm in the
> street.
>
> What does it mean? No light is admitted into the darkened
> chamber, and people unaccustomed to it enter, and, treading softly,
> but heavily, carry a weight into the bedroom and lay it down. (720)

The technique is cinematic: the narrative is conducted by a series of
images, the narrator at this stage offering no more comment than a
camera.

Another death scene, however, indicates that on occasion the narrator is capable of telling as well as showing. At the end of chapter 47
the death of Jo the crossing-sweeper is presented largely through dialogue and laconic metaphorical narrative statement ("The cart is
shaken all to pieces, and the rugged road is very near its end")—until,
that is, the final paragraph, where the narrator seems to step out of the
framework of the scene of which he has been such a close and closely
involved witness: "Dead, your Majesty. Dead, my lords and gentlemen. Dead, Right Reverends and Wrong Reverends of every order.
Dead, men and women, born with Heavenly compassion in your
hearts. And dying thus around us every day (705)." It is as though the
narrator were turning his back on the fictional characters and address-
ing not merely the readers of the novel but the upper and middle
classes of England from the queen downward. The "us" of the final
sentence is significant in its insistence on shared moral responsibility:
the pronoun both promotes discomfort (it is nobody's problem but
ours) and reinforces the idea of connection so central to this novel.

The anonymous narrator's omniscience is incomplete, therefore,
because he often seems to be witnessing a scene that unfolds before his
eyes and, like a sports commentator, to be describing it as it happens.
(Dickens had, of course, been a journalist; his contemporary Walter
Bagehot once remarked in a happy phrase that he wrote "like a special
correspondent for posterity.") Esther's, on the other hand, is a retro-

spective narrative that contains occasional reminders that she is looking back to an earlier epoch of her own life and of public history. When she recalls her journey to the Kent coast, for instance, she mentions that "It was a night's journey in those coach times" (674): many middle-aged readers of this novel, written in the railway age, would make the connection with their own youth "in those coach times."

Esther does not simply look back on the past, however; she comments on the past in the light of subsequent knowledge. When she says of Richard Carstone that "he was postponing his best truth and earnestness . . . until Jarndyce and Jarndyce should be off his mind. Ah me! what Richard would have been without that blight, I never shall know now!" (578), she allows the "present" of the narrative (which, as the tense indicates, is actually past) to be colored by her awareness of what lies in the future in the narrative (which, at the time of narration, belongs to the past). In the following passage, this device serves to heighten the significance of a dramatic moment in the story:

> I had no thought, that night—none, I am quite sure—of what was soon to happen to me. But I have always remembered since, that when we had stopped at the garden-gate to look up at the sky, and when we went upon our way, I had for a moment an undefinable impression of myself as being something different from what I then was. I know it was then, and there, that I had it. I have ever since connected the feeling with that spot and time, and with everything associated with that spot and time, to the distant voices in the town, the barking of a dog, and the sound of wheels coming down the miry hill. (484–85)

The repeated phrase "spot and time" recalls Wordsworth's famous "spots of time," those moments of peculiar awareness that become permanently embedded in the memory, described in his autobiographical poem *The Prelude,* published in 1850; and in the last two passages quoted "then" and "now" are key words. Another passage, later in the novel, suggests that this "foreshadowing" device could also have whetted the curiosity of the readers of a serial: "I could have no anticipation, and I had none, that something very startling to me at the moment, and ever memorable to me in what ensued from it, was to happen before this day was out" (656), where the narrator's earlier ignorance and her later knowledge are simultaneously presented.

Esther is a self-conscious narrator who draws attention to her role, and she makes it clear that it is not altogether a congenial one at the very beginning of her narrative: "I have a great deal of difficulty in beginning to write my portion of these pages." (62). The sense of her sitting, pen in hand, writing her story, is strong. ("There! I have wiped [my tears] away now, and can go on again properly" [66].) She is also conscious of the progress of her task, as in the conclusion of chapter 37: "I look along the road before me, where the distance already shortens and the journey's end is growing visible; and, true and good above the dead sea of the Chancery suit, and all the ashy fruit it cast ashore, I think I see my darling" (592). At the beginning of the final chapter of her narrative she even refers to the reader ("the unknown friend to whom I write").

She is not, however, completely candid with the reader, and there are signs that the writing of the story is imposing something of a strain upon her. Her sentences sometimes falter, as when she admits at the end of chapter 14 that "I have forgotten to mention—at least I have not mentioned" certain matters related to Woodcourt: this is a very sensitive area of her memory, and she touches on it only with difficulty. Again, at the beginning of chapter 30 she describes Mrs. Woodcourt's insinuations ("sometimes she almost made me uncomfortable"), speculates on the origins of her feelings, and concludes, 'I don't know what it was. Or at least if I do, now, I thought I did not then. Or at least—but it don't matter" (467). The relationship between "then" and "now" seems curiously confused: While Esther had every reason to feel uncomfortable at the time, there seems little reason why she should do so when, as Woodcourt's wife, she narrates the story. Dickens is perhaps suggesting that Esther's nature is not such a transparently simple one as it might appear, and that the narrator's role creates genuine difficulties for her.

Or consider the following passage later in the same chapter:

Why could not I . . . not trouble myself about the harmless things [Mrs. Woodcourt] said to me? . . . why should I harp afterwards, with actual distress and pain, on every word she said, and weigh it over again in twenty scales? Why was it so worrying to me to have her in our house . . . ? These were perplexities and contradictions that I could not account for. At least, if I could— but I shall come to all that by and by, and it is mere idleness to go on about it now. (470–71)

As narrator, Esther seems here to be deliberately adopting a kind of limited omniscience about her own past: of course, at the time of the writing, she understands perfectly well why the unspoken intentions of Mrs. Woodcourt disturbed her, but it makes a more effective narrative to pretend that she still feels the anxieties and bafflement of the time. In places, though, the effect of this can be to suggest that Esther has failed to understand herself either earlier or later. When she destroys the flowers Woodcourt has given her, she remarks, "I could have no reason for crying" (669): it is as if her lack of awareness of her own hidden motives has persisted into later life, and for once, in this touching scene, there is no emphasis on the contrast between "then" and "now." The destruction of the flowers parallels the much earlier scene in which she buried her doll—another moment that is perhaps unconsciously self-revealing, and one to which the modern reader will have no difficulty in attaching deep significance.

Although Esther cannot enjoy the unlimited mobility of the anonymous narrator, she does encounter a considerable number of the characters in the novel. Occasionally Dickens resorts to a little contrivance to ensure that she will be present at a particular scene, as in chapter 23, where Prince Turveydrop is reported as asking whether she "could be prevailed upon to be present" (380) when he tells his father that he is engaged to Caddy Jellyby. For all her innocence and naïveté, she is a sharp-eyed observer and capable of being a shrewd judge of and ironic commentator upon character and behavior. This leads us from a consideration of Esther as narrator to a disucssion of her character in broader terms in the next chapter.

7

Women in *Bleak House*

A recent essay on the women characters in *Bleak House* opens with the statement, "It is commonplace to observe that Dickens's view of women is sentimental, sexist, patriarchal, and derogatory," and goes on to quote feminist critic Carolyn Heilbrun as claiming that "there is no arguing with the fact that, in the novels we have, he simply could not conceive of women as complex human beings." The trouble with such a view is not that it is positively wrong but that it fails to take account of or does not sufficiently take into account variations of emphasis found in different novels and in different phases of Dickens's career as a novelist. John C. Ward in fact goes on to argue that the characters of Esther and Lady Dedlock constitute "an interesting exception to the rule" and that their relationship is "a profound comment on the corruption of the patriarchal systems of English law and life."[50]

It is true that most of Dickens's early novels are male dominated. In *Nicholas Nickleby* and *Martin Chuzzlewit,* for instance, he follows the picaresque tradition, as adapted by eighteenth-century English novelists such as Fielding and Smollett (both of whom he had read in childhood), and sends his heroes through a variety of scenes. As the

very titles indicate, the interest is centered firmly on the male protagonist, who is mobile and nomadic in contrast to the majority of the
other characters, including the women, who are static or sedentary.
Even as late as *David Copperfield,* the immediate predecessor of *Bleak
House,* this basic pattern persists. But in *Dombey and Son* a new
emphasis had begun to appear. Here the title is cunningly deceptive,
and the centrality of the male is challenged by life's realities: the son
dies early in the novel, Florence Dombey emerges as the heroine, and,
as one of the minor characters puts it, "Dombey and son is a daughter
after all."

In *Bleak House* Dickens goes even farther and places two women
characters at the center of his story, making one of them—uniquely—a
narrator of half the novel. Nor is there any shortage of lesser female
characters: about twenty women have significant roles, and there are
many others of less importance (such as, for instance, the daughters of
Skimpole, Vholes, and the Bagnets). In this chapter we shall first look
at some of the minor characters and at the ways in which they form
groups and cross-relationships as the novel develops, and then look in
greater detail at Esther and her mother.

First, though, it will be useful to outline Dickens's general attitudes
and assumptions to women, as a background to the consideration of
particular characters. An invaluable guide here is Michael Slater, whose
Dickens and Women has an important chapter on "The Womanly
Ideal." Slater begins by stating, "It was for Dickens a fundamental
belief, as it was for the great majority of his contemporaries, that man's
nature, his psychological and emotional make-up, differed, fundamen-
tally and inherently, from woman's. She was, as Tennyson put it in
1847, 'not undevelopt man,/But diverse.' "[51] For Dickens, among the
distinctively feminine attributes are intuition, deriving from "quickness
of observation," and a capacity for tenderness and pity that qualifies her
both as "a tender of sick minds and bodies" and also as "a sort of
natural priest, closer to God than man, and a source for him of spiritual
strength and encouragement, especially in the face of death." In Christian terms, woman becomes for Dickens and his contemporaries "an
embodiment of the grace and mercy of God." All this, Slater argues, is

"inextricably bound up with [Dickens's] celebrated idealization of the domestic": "It was always in terms of personal relationships, especially within a family grouping, that woman, for him as for most Victorians, realized her full moral and spiritual potential."[52]

This view of women, however, involves both limitations and problems. To quote Slater again, "Dickens's presentation of admirable wives does not rise much above the level of efficient housewifery with much emphasis on the creation of neatness and order, comfort and the provision of plenty of food." (This and some of Slater's other observations can readily be applied to Esther Summerson; he also suggests that "Mrs Bagnet . . . is one of Dickens's few examples of a mature woman functioning admirably as wife and mother.") Moreover, Dickens has "extreme difficulty in reconciling the sexual with the domestic ideal" and has an "apparent nervousness about any manifestation of aggressive female passion (as opposed to passive female devotion)", perhaps because this involves "seeing women as adult human beings rather than as children or as angels." (Again, the application to Lady Dedlock and, less significantly, to Hortense is obvious.) Slater further comments, "Given Dickens's nervousness about seeing women as possessed of a sexual responsiveness equivalent to men's, it is not surprising that he should be so fond . . . of presenting wives as though they were children so that we seem to be reading about fathers and daughters rather than husbands and wives." Finally, Slater notes Dickens's preoccupation with "the idea of natural sisterhood, or female-bonding"; here such relationships as those between Esther and Ada and between Esther and Caddy Jellyby come to mind.[53]

Slater, as we have seen, draws attention to the important role of domestic and family ties in Dickens's presentation of his women characters, and this suggests one way of looking at *Bleak House*. The absence of these ties, and the search for substitutes, can be a rich source of dramatic and psychological interest; and to a large extent this is a novel about deprivation. The two most important characters are a girl who believes herself to be an orphan and a mother who believes her child is dead. Each at last discovers the existence of the other, but not before each finds substitutes or partial substitutes for her missing kin (Esther regards Jarndyce, her guardian, as a father; Lady Dedlock takes a quasi-maternal interest in her maid, Rosa). Ada and Richard are orphans, though they are related to each other (as cousins) and form a closer relationship (as husband and wife); both also form a brotherly/sisterly relationship with Esther. The Neckett children become orphans but are "adopted" by Gridley and Mrs. Blinder; Charley becomes Esther's maid and confidante, and hence a kind of younger sister-by-adoption.

Not all orphans find substitute parents and siblings, though. Jo looks in vain for kindness from Chadband, Skimpole, and Bucket, among others; Snagsby's instincts are partly thwarted by the suspicions of his wife, who believes that he actually *is* the boy's father; and the practical sympathy of George Rouncewell and Allan Woodcourt comes too late. Guster is an orphan who has been brutally treated at the baby-farm and who receives no kindness from her employer, Mrs. Snagsby; she does, however, show a sisterly fellow-feeling for her companion in misfortune, Jo. And some children are orphans not in fact but in effect, through the indifference of their parents (especially their mothers): the Jellyby and Pardiggle children, though they do not suffer the material privations of Jo, are neglected and unhappy. These examples do not exhaust the varieties of deprivation that are illustrated in *Bleak House*. George Rouncewell, for instance, believing that he has disgraced his family, in effect renders himself an orphan by refusing to make contact with his elderly mother; and among the Turveydrops, natural parental love and care are withdrawn from the younger generation and the self-centered old man ruthlessly exploits his son, who thus becomes a kind of orphan.

This novel full of orphans, however, also contains numerous families, from the aristocratic Dedlocks (who are childless but intermittently surrounded by a parasitical extended family) to the brutal brickmaker and his wife, Jenny. Between the two extremes are the middle-class families such as the Jellybys and the Pardiggles. The Bagnets have already been cited as an instance of that rare thing in Dickens's novels, a happy family with responsible and caring parents both alive and well. The Smallweeds present a farcical, almost Beckett-like travesty of family life; and the predatory lawyer Vholes, with his frequent references to his support of an aged father and unmarried daughters, seems to be a parody of familial concern. Finally, the childless bachelor Jarndyce surrounds himself with a substitute family consisting of Esther, Ada, and Richard.

In most of these examples, women play a part; and we can next ask how far their presentation conforms to the limited stereotypes indicated by Slater. As already indicated, there is a considerable *social* range. If some of the middle-class women fall into the familiar Victorian "angel in the house" category, the same cannot be said of Jenny, the brickmaker's wife, who is shown—approvingly but unsentimentally—as rising above appalling conditions of poverty and degradation. Mrs. Bagnet is clearly a more forceful and decisive personality than her husband—though the latter, significantly, insists that "discipline must be maintained" and pretends that his wife is merely the mouthpiece for his own views. These two women, a slum dweller and an army wife, stand outside, or at least on the edge of, the main social world of the novel; and as far as most of the women characters are concerned, their roles are limited, both externally, in the sense that their capacity for action is strictly circumscribed, and internally, in the sense that their psychological natures lack depth.

It is only fair to add, though, that these limitations are not exclusively of Dickens's making but reflect the conditions of his age. Take, for example, the matter of women's occupations. Several women in the novel are servants of different ranks. (Hortense is a lady's maid, as is Rosa; Guster is a maid of all work, as is Charley Neckett until Esther rescues her from the Smallweeds and makes her her own personal maid). Apart from the servants, a very large class in Dickens's England, very few female occupations are represented. The Miss Donny twins are teachers, and Esther prepares to become a governess—for teaching was one of the very few occupations open to middle-class women (and its rewards and social status were, of course, very low).

What causes much more uneasiness among Dickens's readers and critics is his attitude toward women who want to engage in the man's world of action and, by their own energies and efforts, help to make the world a better place. One possible means for a woman to do this in the mid-nineteenth century was to engage in philanthropic activities; and one of Dickens's friends at this time was Angela Burdett Coutts, later Baroness Coutts, a member of a prominent banking family and reputedly the richest unmarried woman in England. Dickens worked with her and for her in her charitable enterprises; his biographer Edgar Johnson has said that Dickens "became the guiding conscience of her philanthropic career." Dickens's numerous letters to her indicate that his respect and admiration for her were considerable; there was clearly no question but that she was behaving entirely properly.

Why, then, are Mrs. Jellyby and, to a lesser extent, Mrs. Pardiggle the targets of Dickens's merciless satire in *Bleak House?* For Dickens, a woman's proper role is that of wife and mother. Unmarried women are either comical, like Judy Smallweed (whose first name is that of the grotesque doll in the traditional Punch and Judy show), or pathetic, like Miss Flite (whose name suggests "flighty" in the sense of "mentally unstable"). Even childless couples like the Snagsbys and the Chadbands are depicted as eccentric. "Normal" women are either those who are already wives and mothers or those who are waiting, like Esther and Rosa, for marriage and motherhood. Such a destiny is seen as offering a woman complete fulfillment and a complete occupation. But in pursuing their respective missions, Mrs. Jellyby and Mrs. Pardiggle neglect their primary duties; the former's home in particular is shown as a scene of chaos, and her numerous children, from little Peepy to Caddy, who is of marriageable age, are woefully neglected. Mr. Jellyby is in despair, and as a result of his wife's fecklessness, his financial affairs are desperate.

There are some curious implications in all this. It does not seem to have occurred to Dickens that it might be possible for a woman to run her home and family efficiently and simultaneously to have interests outside the home; or if it occurred to him, he does not take it into account. The portrayal of Mrs. Jellyby is, therefore, to some extent one-sided. Moreover, it has the effect of ridiculing her cause, which is the organization of emigration to West Africa and the spreading of civilization among the natives. Whilst our own generation is less sympathetic to, and more suspicious of, the intentions and motives of colonizers, this was, in Victorian terms, a far from absurd undertaking; yet Dickens treats it as if it were a huge joke—as, in the novel, it becomes, thanks to the seductive power of Dickens's comedy. Still, the problem of the energetic woman (and Mrs. Jellyby is certainly that) who cannot find full satisfaction in the home has not been faced. No wonder John Stuart Mill, a contemporary of Dickens and an ardent defender of the rights of women, was infuriated by *Bleak House* and in particular by "the vulgar impudence" on Dickens's part in "ridicul-[ing] rights of women."[54]

At the same time, we must return to the fact that women occupy a central place in this novel. A modern feminist critic, Ellen Moers, has detected a fundamental inconsistency: on the surface, Dickens is antagonistic to the claims for women's freedom that were being made at this time (and that were to gather momentum as the century wore on), but on a more profound level he shows an awareness that his earlier conceptions and presentations of feminine psychology are inadequate. Moers suggests that the women in *Bleak House* are "more forceful, more independent, more capable" than those in other novels.[55] These epithets can certainly be applied with confidence to Lady Dedlock; whether they can also be applied to Esther Summerson is much more arguable. To these two major characters we now turn.

Honoria Dedlock (her first name is both classically elegant and ironic) is that familiar figure of Victorian melodrama, a woman with a past. Physically, she resembles characters in other novels who fulfill a somewhat similar role (for example, Edith in *Dombey and Son*): beautiful, elegant, an imposing and statuesque figure (she "has the effect of being tall," 58), with a haughty manner that does not readily show feeling. She is richly dressed and "at the top of the fashionable tree" (57). But having conquered the fashionable world, she is, as she declares on her first appearance, "bored to death" (56): "An exhausted composure, a worn-out placidity, an equanimity of fatigue not to be ruffled by interest or satisfaction, are the trophies of her victory. She is perfectly well-bred. If she could be translated to Heaven to-morrow, she might be expected to ascend without any rapture" (57–58). In the course of the novel, this dignity and composure give way to fear, despair, panic, flight, and death; and the power game played by Tulkinghorn, in which she is a victim, and her discovery of Esther's existence are told with great narrative power.

Her affair with Captain Hawdon, which led to the birth of Esther long before the action of the novel opens, shows her to be a woman of deep feelings who is prepared to behave unconventionally when her passions are aroused; and her behavior as Lady Dedlock is plainly an attempt to suppress (Dickens uses the metaphor of freezing) that side of her nature. Psychologically, the situation is an interesting one, but the reader gains very little insight into her inner life, and as a result Lady Dedlock too often seems stagey and improbable in her speech and behavior. When, disguised as a servant, she persuades Jo to show her the foul churchyard where her lover lies buried, her language and actions convey nothing of whatever real emotions she might be supposed to be feeling:

> "Go before me, and show me all those dreadful places. Stop opposite to each, and don't speak to me unless I speak to you. Don't look back. Do what I want, and I will pay you well.". . .
> "I'm fly," says Jo. "But fen larks, you know! Stow hooking it!"
> "What does the horrible creature mean?" exclaims the servant, recoiling from him. (277)

When she learns that she has been deceived into thinking that her child is dead, and when she later finds that Tulkinghorn means to betray her secret when it suits him to do so, she gives way to emotion privately even though she maintains her glacial manner in public. But her emotions are depicted through the stylized gestures of the melodramatic stage (striding up and down, tearing her hair, flinging herself on the ground), so that again there is no sense of inwardness in Dickens's treatment of this character—no glimpse of what it actually might have been like to *be* Lady Dedlock, or any woman (and there must have been many in the past) who had been deprived of her child and of the man she loved and was compelled to maintain appearances without ever knowing the relief of sharing her secret with anyone. It comes as no surprise to find that a four-act play titled *Lady Dedlock's Secret*, adapted from Dickens's novel, was later produced in London.

Lady Dedlock, then, is certainly one of Dickens's "strong" women characters, but in the end she remains a stereotype. The opportunity to explore the workings of sexual passion and sexual guilt, or to represent the effects of suppression and misery, is not taken. If Dickens contemplated doing so, he might well have been deterred by considerations of prudence, for he was after all writing a serial for family consumption. (When Thomas Hardy, later in the century, made bolder and franker attempts to deal with questions of sex and marriage, he encountered serious opposition from publishers, editors, critics, and readers.) In any case, though, Dickens for once failed to find a language appropriate to the character and her situation. Marvelously inventive and endlessly various as he can be in devising individual modes of speech for his comic characters, faced with a wholly serious character such as Lady Dedlock, Dickens falls back on theatrical conventions. Her accidental view of her dead lover's handwriting is a telling dramatic moment, but we see her, as we see a character on the stage, only from the outside: " 'Faint,' my lady murmurs, with white lips, 'only that; but it is like the faintness of death. Don't speak to me. Ring, and take me to my room!" Again, after she learns from Guppy that her daughter is living, she delivers a soliloquy that could have come straight from the script of some indifferent Victorian melodrama: " 'O my child, my child! Not dead in the first hours of her life, as my cruel sister told me; but sternly nurtured by her, after she had renounced me and my name! O my child, O my child!' " (466). The formality and conventionality of the language ("sternly nurtured") is curiously at odds with the supposed emotions. No less conventional is her behavior after the dramatic interview with Tulkinghorn in his tower room: "pacing her own rooms with her hair wildly thrown from her flung-back face, her hands clasped behind her head, her figure twisted as if by pain" (638). Esther Summerson's observation that Mr. Turveydrop lacked "nature" can be applied with equal appropriateness to her mother.

Women in Bleak House

If the trouble with Lady Dedlock is that a potentially interesting character is oversimplified, the problem with Esther is that she may be too complex, may have led Dickens into ambiguities and inconsistencies, and, according to some critics, may have got out of hand. She has been much more widely discussed than any other character in the novel, and she has provoked widely divergent views and interpretations. I have suggested in the previous chapter that Dickens took great pains to differentiate as sharply as possible between the language and the tone of his two narrators, and while the novel was in the process of composition, he wrote to a young American correspondent that it was costing him "no little labor and anxiety"[56] to write a distinctively feminine narrative. The same letter inquires, "Is it quite natural, quite girlish?" but the "girlishness" is precisely what some critics and readers have found distasteful. For them Esther is coy, sentimental, excessively self-effacing, and irritatingly self-righteous as she jingles her keys and spreads sweetness and light among all she encounters. In Michael Slater's phrase, she is for such readers "an exasperating paragon of female virtue."[57]

Such complaints about Esther began very early. A reviewer in the *Spectator* expressed the wish that "she would either do something spicy or confine herself to superintending the jam-pots at Bleak House,"[58] and Charlotte Brontë found her "too often weak and twaddling."[59] There is, however, an entirely different view of Esther that has been advanced by some modern interpreters of this novel, usefully summarized by Slater:

[She is] a character who has been severely damaged psychologically by a loveless childhood and whose narration is marked by emotional and psychological peculiarities which show the abiding scars. Esther's constant self-deprecation, her apparently desperate desire to be incessantly busy and useful to others, her idolization of Ada, her willing acceptance of the Dame Durden little-old-woman role in Jarndyce's household, her fierce reaction to Guppy's coarse nuptial overtures, her total confusion over her attraction to Alan Woodcourt and his to her, her strange hallucinations when dangerously ill, the complexity of her response to Jarndyce's sexless marriage-proposal, all these things, and many other touches in the narrative, may be seen as creating a coherent and convincing impression of a neurotic personality.[60]

Slater goes on to define the neurosis in question as "the kind in which the sufferer is always struggling with a crushing sense of his or her own total worthlessness and is virtually paralysed with regard to any conscious assertion of personal needs, desires, beliefs and feelings."

When a character provokes such opposing views—is the portrayal of Esther shallow, conventional, and tedious or complex and psychologically penetrating?—it can be supposed that one of two things has happened. Either some readers have brought to the text a subtlety and ingenuity that has detected qualities overlooked by the more perfunctory reading of others, or the writer himself has not fully resolved the creative problems posed by the character and has given us a text marred by inconsistencies. These difficulties are bound up with the fact that Esther tells her own story and is the chief witness for her own virtues. Some critics have argued that Dickens ultimately failed to solve the problems posed by his highly original and experimental narrative method. According to Slater, "Dickens seems . . . to be trying to make Esther function both as an unreliable and as a reliable narrator at the same time and the result is, not surprisingly, unsatisfactory"[61]; and Hawthorn similarly concludes that "Dickens had not successfully fixed the technical aspects of Esther's narrative."[62]

A large part of the trouble is, of course, that there are *two* Esthers: the character (in the novel's present) and the narrator (writing at a moment in which the action of the novel has receded into the past). This has led critic Michael S. Kearns to refer to "the difficulty of writing about *Bleak House,* especially if the writer is going to use the convention of speaking about the story in the present. This convention does not allow the writer sufficient access to the subtle relationship between Esther's "story" and her "discourse," between what she tells and how she tells it."[63] Part of the difference between "what she tells and how she tells it" is a difference of time, since the action of the novel and Esther's composition of her narrative are separated by a number of years. The two Esthers are thus differentiated in age, status (single and dependent versus married), and personal maturity. One way of reading Esther's portion of the novel—and perhaps even of resolving some of the apparent inconsistencies—is to take full account of this double perspective in the same way that is done in reading Dickens's later first-person narrative in *Great Expectations,* where the hero-narrator frequently draws attention to the then-and-now, the myself-as-I-was-and-as-I-am aspect of his story.

Consider, for instance, the apparent disparity between Esther's innocence and inexperience (that is, that of the *younger* Esther) and the not infrequently shrewd and penetrating comments made upon characters such as Skimpole and Turveydrop. W. F. Axton has pointed out in an influential essay that, while Esther repeatedly denies any pretensions to cleverness, she has "the most acute insight" of anyone in the novel and often appears in the role of the "detached observer who sees with devastating precision."[64] Axton suggests that this is a deliberate attempt on Dickens's part to imply a conflict in Esther's nature and hence to present her as a more complex and interesting character than just another simpering and insipid girl-heroine. It might equally well be argued, however, that the two aspects reflect Esther's two roles: the more sophisticated and self-aware mature woman recreates an earlier stage of her own existence and, with benefit of hindsight, comments, from the standpoint of mature judgment, on matters she did not fully understand at the time.

Near the beginning of her narrative, for instance, when Esther states that in her childhood she "had never heard my mama spoken of" (63), there is no hint of the knowledge concerning her mother that Esther later acquires—knowledge still far ahead in the time-scheme of the novel but long familiar to the narrating Esther, who withholds the information at this point. A few pages later Esther writes that "Mrs. Rachael was too good to feel any emotion at parting, but I was not so good, and wept bitterly" (69). Here again the mature Esther pretends to share the ignorance and innocence of the young girl she once was: the older woman knows, as the reader knows, that Mrs. Rachael was not "too good" but too cold and indifferent.

At some points in her narrative Esther's style changes abruptly: instead of the simple, candid, and rather unworldly prose established for Esther at the outset and fairly consistently maintained, we find an astringent wit much more like that of Dickens's third-person narrators—and that of Dickens himself. In chapter 38, for instance, describing the apprentices at Turveydrop's dancing academy, she writes: "Returning with their jackets buttoned, and their pumps stuck in them, they then produced packets of cold bread and meat, and bivouacked under a painted lyre on the wall" (596). The uncommon word "bivouacked" and the fanciful detail of the "painted lyre" seem to belong to a manner quite different from Esther's. Later, Mrs. Guppy is described as "holding her pocket-handkerchief to her chest, like a fomentation, with both hands"; and here again the comic simile is characteristically Dickensian. the obvious explanation here is that Dickens has temporarily forgotten to maintain the "girlish" manner he has prescribed for himself and has allowed this touch of wit— delightful in itself but surely out of character—to slip in.

At other times, however, Esther shows a genuine shrewdness in judging character and motive. Faced with such fraudulent figures as Skimpole and Turveydrop, she is quick to detect the hollowness of their pretensions. She also acts as a remarkably efficient camera-eye in recording the individual aspects of those she meets; one of the earliest critics of the novel, a reviewer in the *Athenaeum* on 17 September 1853, acknowledged this in praising the accuracy of her observation and finding in her "the immediate power of the daguerrotype [a kind of early photograph] in noting at once the minutest singularities of so many exceptional people."[65] Her capacity in this respect increases as the novel progresses; and while so many characters are static and unvarying, Esther grows and matures in the course of the story.

In many passages, indeed, her apparently artless narrative conveys a sense of the complexity of her own emotions and the internal conflicts she is suffering, even when these are not directly articulated. This is especially obvious in relation to her gradually growing feelings for Allan Woodcourt. The placing of her early reference to him is of interest: at the end of chapter 13, which is also the end of the fourth monthly number, he is mentioned as "a gentleman of a dark complexion—a young surgeon" (233), whom Esther finds on first encounter to be "very sensible and agreeable." The apparently casual and low-key allusion to Woodcourt, not yet named, is belied by the placing of the paragraph in such a conspicuous and emphatic position, whereby the serial reader could hardly have helped wondering what further role this sensible and agreeable young man was to play. In the much-later chapter 44, in which Esther receives and accepts Jarndyce's proposal of marriage, her narrative again feigns an incomprehension that belongs to the young girl she then is but that can hardly have been shared by the older woman recalling the past. Reading Jarndyce's letter, it is "as if something for which there was no name or distinct idea were indefinitely lost to me" (668), and, weeping over the withered flowers that were Woodcourt's gift and that she had carefully and revealingly kept, Esther puts them to the lips of the sleeping Ada: "I thought about her love for Richard; though, indeed, the flowers had nothing to do with that" (668–69). Naturally the narrator would have no difficulty in attaching a "name or distinct idea" to these obscure emotions; but to do so would be to destroy the delicate and psychologically interesting presentation of Esther's state of mind.

Esther, then, knows more than she tells, and her reasons for not telling are themselves of interest. This is not simply a matter of narrative technique but is related to the portrayal of Esther as the major character of the novel. (At the outset, she confesses that "It seems so curious to me to be obliged to write all this about myself! As if this narrative were the narrative of *my* life!" [74]; but though the narrative is certainly other things too, that is surely what it primarily is). The older view of Esther as excessively and childishly naïve, representative of a patronizing conception of the role and capacities of women, is shared by few modern critics, though A. E. Dyson has produced an interesting interpretation that sees Esther, "the harbinger of domestic virtue, happiness and peace," as "a gravitational pull against pessimism and defeatism" in a novel whose world "remains tragic."[66] Esther is no stereotype but a complex individual whose portrayal raises questions not only about character but about what happens when we remember and try to reproduce the past. Paul Eggert has argued that "Dickens had committed himself to a psychological study deeper, probably, than he had anticipated and more complex, finally, than he could handle"[67]; and the view that Esther is not realized with complete success is shared by other critics. Her complexity does, however, suggest that at this stage in his career Dickens was taking more seriously the problems of presenting women characters in fiction, and perhaps also that, outside fiction, his attitudes to women were undergoing modification. Esther can be seen as one of the first—and probably *the* first—of a line of more ambitious and subtle studies of women in his later novels: Amy Dorrit, Estella in *Great Expectations*, Bella Wilfer in *Our Mutual Friend*, and others.

8

The Language of
Bleak House

To speak of the language of *Bleak House* is to be guilty of a gross oversimplification, for this wonderfully diverse, dense, and panoramic novel contains not one language but many. In it we find a polyphony of "voices" belonging to the narrators and the characters, and these are so sharply distinguished from each other that the reader can never, for instance, mistake the language of Skimpole for that of Jarndyce, while such characters as Chadband and Turveydrop and Tulkinghorn (and dozens of others) are differentiated as much by their speech as by their physical appearance.

Here, it should be noted, we encounter a paradox that is central to Dickens's unique achievement. It comes quite naturally to refer to "voices" and "speech" in discussing a novel such as *Bleak House,* but it is after all, and always has been, a *written* text, and the distinctive or eccentric "sounds" that the reader may "hear" in the course of reading are generated exclusively by written symbols—by black marks on white paper. And yet there are good grounds for insisting on the *oral* element in Dickens's art and style. His lifelong passion for the theater led him to introduce a strongly dramatic element into his fiction and perhaps to "perform" roles and scenes as he conceived and composed his novels. In the last twelve years of his life he enjoyed a second and highly successful career as a reader of his own work to large and enthusiastic audiences in Britain and America—evidence that his writings lend themselves readily to performance. Furthermore, many would have encountered his stories through the ear rather than through the eye, for reading aloud was a well-established practice in Victorian families. This oral element should be kept in mind in considering Dickens as a stylist.

The most prominent "voices" in this novel are those of the two narrators, and something has been said earlier about the pains Dickens took to mark the contrasts between them in tense, vocabulary, and tone. Alone among Dickens's novels, *Bleak House* provides frequent alternations between contrasting narrative voices. Within these narratives, there are the *idiolects* or individual modes of speech of a very large number of characters, and Dickens's dialogue provides more variety than any other element in his work. A character's speech may carry simultaneously two different kinds of signals or markers: those that proclaim his or her individuality or uniqueness, and those indicating membership of a social, occupational, or other group. Many of the characters in *Bleak House* are given modes of speech that carry both of these elements.

In his *Preface to Shakespeare's Works* (1725) Alexander Pope said of Shakespeare's plays that "had all the Speeches been printed without the very names of the Persons, I believe one might have apply'd them with certainty to every speaker," and this is one of several qualities that Dickens shares with Shakespeare. It would be difficult to name two characters in the novel whose speeches could be interchanged, and there are many whose identity is immediately obvious from the internal evidence of their dialogue. This was not merely a fictional convention but a recognition on Dickens's part of what is accepted by modern students of language: that even people who have much in common do not speak in an identical manner but draw individually on the vast resources of the language.

In a few of the characters of *Bleak House,* indeed, life and fiction meet, since Dickens is known to have based them on actual persons known to him. Skimpole, for instance, is a portrait of the writer Leigh Hunt (1784–1859). In a letter to a friend written on 25 September 1853 (that is, soon after finishing the novel) Dickens confessed: "I suppose [Skimpole] is the most exact portrait that was ever painted in words! . . . the likeness is astonishing. I don't think it could possibly be more like [Hunt]. It is so awfully true that I make a bargain with myself 'never to do so any more.' There is not an atom of exaggeration or suppression. It is an absolute reproduction of a real man." The portrait was quickly recognized by readers, and one critic wrote: "I recognized Skimpole instantaneously; . . . and so did every person whom I talked with about it who had ever had Leigh Hunt's acquaintance."[68]

What is known of Hunt's manner of speech suggests that Dickens was imitating it closely, along with much else. One lady who knew Hunt recalled that "he had taken her into the garden, and talked to her, and asked her what she thought heaven would be like, and then he said, 'I will tell you what I think it will be like: I think it will be like a most beautiful arbour all hung with creepers and flowers, and that one will be able to sit in it all day, and read a most interesting novel.' "[69] This seems very close to the fanciful, self-indulgent, and irresponsible manner of the character in the novel.

Boythorn is another character based on well-documented actuality. Veteran author Walter Savage Landor (1775–1864) was well known to Dickens, who named his second son after him; again, contemporaries were quick to perceive that Dickens had included an affectionately teasing portrait of his friend in the novel. Critic Henry Crabb Robinson remarked that Landor's "fierce tones, tenderness of heart, and exaggeration in all his judgments [are] described with great truth and force"[70] in the character of Boythorn. It is interesting that both Hunt and Landor were much older than Dickens and were survivors from an earlier period, that of the Romantic poets; they thus have an appropriate place in a novel that looks back in time and depicts a number of characters (Sir Leicester Dedlock, Mr. Turveydrop, and others) and institutions (notably the Court of Chancery) that are anachronisms.

As these examples suggest, Dickens drew on real life in his efforts to endow characters with individual modes of speech. He also drew on his wide observation, aided by a very acute ear and a passionate interest in language, of the speech habits of different groups within English society. From the upper-class speech habits of the Dedlocks and their relatives to the debased English spoken by the uneducated Jo, who says "inkwich" for "inquest" and "consequential" for "consecrated," the dialogue in *Bleak House* covers the entire range of urban society. It has been suggested earlier that some of the most dramatic scenes occur when representatives of different social levels come face to face; in these scenes the dialogue can play an important part in stressing the social gulf. Thus the stiff hereditary dignity of Sir Leicester encounters the bluntness of the unapologetically self-made iron-master; Sir Leicester, again, meets the powerful but socially nondescript Bucket; and most dramatically of all, Lady Dedlock interrogates Jo in a scene in chapter 16 that brings together the extremes of the social scale:

"Do what I want, and I will pay you well."

"I'm fly," says Jo. "But fen larks, you know! Stow hooking it!"

"What does the horrible creature mean?" exclaims [Lady Dedlock], recoiling from him.

"Stow cutting away, you know!" says Jo.

"I don't understand you. . . ." (277)

Quite literally, Jo's language, with its lower-class slang (e.g., "hooking it" for "running away"), is incomprehensible to the aristocratic lady: the barriers not only of wealth and status and dress but also of language are between them. Dickens's manuscript shows that in revising this passage he was careful to stress the slang element in Jo's speech: for "fen larks," for instance, he originally wrote "no larks," just as an earlier Standard English phrase "half a crown" was revised to the slang phrase "half a bull." There is contemporary evidence that Dickens was close to reality in his presentation of Jo's speech, for the great social observer Henry Mayhew (another friend of Dickens's), in his monumental *London Labour and the London Poor* (1851), reported a crossing-sweeper as telling him, "When we are talking together we always talk in a kind of slang."[71]

Apart from exploiting the different speech modes of the whole gamut of urban society, Dickens draws on the distinctive habits of particular pursuits and professions to create what may be referred to as occupational dialects. (Shakespeare's Sonnet 111, quoted in Dickens's "Preface to the First Edition" [41], is relevant to this point: "My nature is subdued / To what it works in, like the dyer's hand. . . .') Consider, for instance, the way in which the numerous representatives of the legal profession are marked by their callings. Turveydrop, Kenge, and Vholes speak differently from each other, but all share a "legal" manner of speech that is dry, formal, unimpassioned, and somewhat pedantic. Even the comic figure of Guppy cannot resist intruding legal terms into private conversation, as when he explains to Esther,

> "What follows is without prejudice, miss?". . .
> "I don't understand what you mean," said I, wondering.
> "It's one of our law terms, miss. You won't make any use of it to my detriment, at Kenge and Carboy's, or elsewhere. . . ." (174)

Some of Dickens's contemporary critics regarded the individualization in his dialogue as too much of a good thing. H. F. Chorley's comment in the *Athenaeum* that there was "progress in exaggeration to be deprecated" in *Bleak House* has been quoted in chapter 4. Similar comments were made at other stages of his career: on one occasion, for instance, the *Saturday Review* complained of his characters that "not one . . . ever subsides into the commonplace speech of real life." Half a century later George Bernard Shaw was to say of *Hard Times,* the novel that followed *Bleak House,* that 'here he begins at last to exercise quite recklessly the power of presenting a character to you in the most fantastic and outrageous terms, putting into its mouth from one end of the book to the other hardly one word which could conceivably be uttered by any sane human being."[72] The modern reader, however, is likely to appreciate more unreservedly the infinite variety of Dickens's dialogue with its rich eccentricity and inexhaustible inventiveness.

Stylistically, the dialogue is the most varied component of the novel, but it is not the only component worthy of attention. Dickens's descriptive writing, whether describing persons or places, can be subtly evocative and incisively effective. The atmosphere of the London streets, especially of the slums, is powerfully created; but from time to time there are contrastive pictures of Chesney Wold, the Dedlock country house, in its rural tranquillity and in the variety of its seasonal moods. The first of these occurs near the beginning of chapter 2, where the passage beginning "The waters are out in Lincolnshire" (56) merits close reading. Notice the poetic precision of the words and the reliance on sound as well as meaning in this passage: "An arch of the bridge in the park has been *sapped* and *sopped* away"; ". . . the soft *loppings* and prunings of the woodman's axe can make no *crash* or *crackle* as they fall" (emphases added). The precision of language is matched by the exactness of visual and aural observation: "The deer, looking soaked, leave quagmires where they pass. The shot of a rifle loses its sharpness in the moist air, and its smoke moves in a tardy little cloud. . . ."

Nor is it simply a set-piece description of the external scene, for—using a familiar device that Ruskin only four years later was to label the "pathetic fallacy"—the visible world is presented as an extension of the mood of the depressive Lady Dedlock, who is, as she puts it, "bored to death." In this respect she resembles the maidens in Tennyson's early poems, such as the heroine of his "Mariana," and it is worth recalling that Dickens was a great admirer of Tennyson's early work (he read the important 1842 collection with enthusiasm), that Lincolnshire, where the Dedlock house is situated, was Tennyson's county, and that there are both a general resemblance of atmosphere and specific verbal parallels (e.g., "dreary") between this passage and a characteristically Tennysonian piece such as "Mariana." In this and other descriptions of Chesney Wold the writing may fairly be described as poetic in its exploitation of the resources of language: in diction and syntax, imagery and sound. Consider, from chapter 29, a single sentence: "Howls the shrill wind round Chesney Wold; the sharp rain beats, the windows rattle, and the chimneys growl" (456), in which the writing draws even closer to verse in that it is strongly metrical.

For an example of character-description we can turn to Dickens's introduction of Mr. Turveydrop in chapter 14:

> He was a fat old gentleman with a false complexion, false teeth, false whiskers, and a wig. He had a fur collar, and he had a padded breast to his coat, which only wanted a star or a broad blue ribbon to be complete. He was pinched in, and swelled out, and got up, and strapped down, as much as he could possibly bear. He had such a neckcloth on (puffing his very eyes out of their natural shape), and his chin and even his ears so sunk into it, that it seemed as though he must inevitably double up, if it were cast loose. He had, under his arm, a hat of great size and weight, shelving downward from the crown to the brim; and in his hand a pair of white gloves, with which he flapped it, as he stood poised on one leg, in a high-shouldered, round-elbowed state of elegance not to be surpassed. He had a cane, he had an eye-glass, he had a snuff-box, he had rings, he had wristbands, he had everything but any touch of nature; he was not like youth, he was not like age, he was not like anything in the world but a model of Deportment. (242–44)

The description proceeds by enumerating separate features and objects: complexion, teeth, whiskers, wig, collar, neckcloth, hat, gloves, cane, eyeglass, snuffbox, rings, and so forth. The same kind of sentence-pattern is repeated over and over again: "He was . . . He had . . . and he had . . . ," and so on. The effect of this is to make the description sound like an inventory or catalog. Dickens does this quite deliberately because it is the artificiality and moral hollowness of Turveydrop that he wishes obliquely to convey: the character is nothing *but* externals, most of them detachable (so that one wonders with a shudder what the old man looks like at night after he has removed the day's finery and falsities).

This view of Turveydrop, however, is implicit, not stated; what the passage does is to insist on the discreteness or separateness of the items enumerated. Rhetorically, the main device used is repetition, both in the syntactical patterns (already noted) and in the vocabulary ("false," for instance, occurs three times in the first sentence). This is a rhetorical style, like that of a popular orator; for a novelist it is also a highly experimental style, the like of which is not found in Dickens's contemporaries such as Thackeray and the Brontës. For another example of the use of repetition, the description of Vholes in chapter 39 (603), with its relentless reiteration of the word "respectable" in such a way as to render it ironic, may be examined.

Dickens's style is indeed experimental and innovative in many ways. One of the most remarkable is the free and flexible way in which narrative, description, and dialogue are merged rather than, as in most novels of the period, kept distinct. In chapter 5, in a discussion of the topical sources of *Bleak House,* I quoted a passage from the cross-examination of George Ruby, the prototype of Jo, as reported in the weekly *Examiner.* The form of the dialogue is the familiar question-and-answer, customary in transcripts of court proceedings. But in chapter 11 of the novel, where Dickens renders a similar dialogue, his method is very different:

> Says the Coroner, is that boy here? Says the beadle, no, sir, he is not here. Says the Coroner, go and fetch him then. In the absence of the active and intelligent, the Coroner converses with Mr. Tulkinghorn.
> O! Here's the boy, gentlemen!
> Here he is, very muddy, very hoarse, very ragged. Now, boy!— But stop a minute. Caution, This boy must be put through a few preliminary paces.
> Name, Jo. Nothing else that he knows on. Don't know that everybody has two names. Never heerd of sich a think. Don't know that Jo is short for a longer name. Thinks it long enough for *him. He* don't find no fault with it. Spell it. No *He* can't spell it. No father, no mother, no friends. Never been to school. What's home? Knows a broom's a broom, and knows it's wicked to tell a lie. Don't recollect who told him about the broom, or about the lie, but knows both. Can't exactly say what'll be done to him arter he's dead if he tells a lie to the gentlemen here, but believes it'll be something wery bad to punish him, and serve him right—and so he'll tell the truth."

The Language of Bleak House

"This won't do, gentlemen!" says the Coroner, with a melancholy shake of the head. (199)

Dickens dispenses with indications of speaker and quotation marks, running Jo's replies together and leaving the reader to infer the questions. He also interpolates narrative and descriptive elements (as in the six-word description of Jo's physical state). The result is to achieve considerable pace and emphasis: the compression makes the episode more dramatic, and the spotlight is firmly on Jo, the central figure.

Two other aspects of Dickens's language call for comment. Dickens had learned from Shakespeare (especially Shakespearean tragedy) the value of recurring images in giving unity to a complex work. There are major and minor images in *Bleak House*: the fog that swirls and seeps from the very first page, the imprisoned wild birds kept by Miss Flite, the spontaneous combustion that causes the death of Krook, the fever that originates in Tom-all-Alone's and infects the middle-class world of Esther, and the East Wind to which Jarndyce so frequently refers, are some of the most obvious. Some of these, such as Miss Flite's birds, can seem to a modern reader a little schematic and self-conscious, but the best of them have considerable power. The fog is both a vividly actualized phenomenon of the London climate (a combination of river mist and smog from the thousands of coal-burning fires in the city) and an apt symbol for the impenetrable obscurities of the law. It can be objected that Dickens is a shade too explicit in pointing to the meaning of his symbol—"at the very heart of the fog, sits the Lord High Chancellor in his High Court of Chancery" (50)—but it should be remembered that his readers had not been trained by twentieth-century literature to respond readily to such devices, and Dickens in a sense had to instruct them in how to read a new kind of novel. We read Dickens with more insight for having read T. S. Eliot and other modernist authors, but in its way *Bleak House* is as original and experimental as *The Waste Land* of some seventy years later.

Finally, Dickens's namings of places and especially of people are a specialized but deeply interesting aspect of his linguistic inventiveness. In Dickens's early novels the significance of names is sometimes crudely transparent: Verisopht for a foolish aristocrat, Crackit for a housebreaker, Sowerberry for an undertaker. Later, however, he took greater pains to produce a more subtly suggestive kind of name, and *Bleak House* contains some of these. By a kind of sound-symbolism, Squod, for instance, suggests the character's deformities, while Vholes is in an obscure way an eerie and disturbing name (perhaps because the combination *Vh* is never found in English words). Krook is a name as bizarre as its owner; it is hard to take very seriously anyone called Turveydrop, Pardiggle, Jellyby, or Guppy; Smallweed belongs to a group of farcical characters, just as surely as Woodcourt has dignified associations that fit with a hero. A few names have a more obvious appropriateness, like Bucket for the deep-thinking detective and Bagnet (bayonet) for a soldier.

All of this suggests a willingness, even an eagerness, to experiment and to exploit the resources of language. Dickens was not inhibited by the kinds of style normally deemed appropriate to prose fiction but drew on the full resources of English and used a variety of new techniques. He needs to be read with this kind of awareness. Often the effectiveness of a passage is increased by the simple procedure of reading it aloud. As a distinguished Shakespeare scholar, Alfred B. Harbage, has said, "If we bring to the reading of Dickens the kind of high expectation and attentiveness we bring to the reading of Shakespeare, we shall not be disappointed. . . . If Shakespeare could have read Dickens, he would have been astonished to learn that this poet had ever been considered anything else."[73]

9

Conclusion

A great novel is not to be fully "understood" after a single reading or even perhaps after the successive readings of a lifetime. There will always be something new to find in it, and each reading seems different from the earlier ones; for like a person, a book seems to show different aspects to us at different times, and we should no more expect to reach a final decision, to "make up our mind" about it, than we do with regard to a member of our family or a close friend.

This short study of *Bleak House* has raised many questions, but it has made no attempt to provide conclusive answers to them all. The reader or student will wish to test the ideas put forward here against his or her own impressions and reactions and to return again and again to the text in order to reread and perhaps reinterpret Dickens's words. The present book will have served its purpose if it has provided some basic information to enable informed judgments to be made and if it has drawn attention to some of the questions that can be most fruitfully asked—for, as the ancient Greeks knew very well, the beginning of wisdom is not to find answers but to ask the right questions.

Perhaps the most remarkable thing about *Bleak House* is the way in which it contrives to be simultaneously historical and universal, a tract for the times and a diagnosis of the human condition. At some stages of this study, especially in chapter 5, I have sought to show how deeply the novel is rooted in the months and years of its composition and publication, and that Dickens's first readers (and they were very numerous) would have responded to it with a shock of recognition as they encountered in the fiction issues that were also being debated in the newspapers and before Parliament. We cannot do better than to read *Bleak House* if we wish to have a sense of what it was like to live in early Victorian England: not merely to share the ideas, hopes, and anxieties of the age, but to perceive with the senses what it was like to walk the streets of London, to stumble through a dense fog (what Guppy described to Esther as "a London particular"), to enter the homes of the rich and the poor, and to see a vast variety of figures, representing many classes and dozens of occupations, both in their representativeness and in their individuality—and not only to see but to *hear,* for Dickens is, along with so much else, the supreme master of fictional dialogue in all its varieties.

At the same time *Bleak House* is not just a museum, though it is an enthralling one. Beneath its contemporary relevance lie fundamental and permanent human problems of the individual and of society. The Court of Chancery has been reformed, but bureaucracy and the slow workings of the machinery of justice are always with us. Our society no longer condemns individuals so harshly for an accident of birth, but Esther Summerson's struggle for self-realization and her yearning to love and be loved are experienced over and over again by individuals in all epochs, not exclusively by Victorian maidens in ankle-length dresses. The crossing-sweeper is no longer a familiar figure in city streets, but the problems of urban filth and pollution (of which the fog is another aspect) have not disappeared. Nor have poverty and suffering disappeared, nor (sadly) the selfishness and indifference that fail to respond to them; and the counterparts of Jo are still (in the words of the narrator as he points an accusing finger at the reader) "dying thus around us every day."

It is in the very nature of fiction to deal with the specific, the contingent, the here and now: novels must be set in particular places

Conclusion

and particular times, and must present highly individualized characters. The great achievement of *Bleak House* is that it not only does all
this supremely well but at the same time speaks to the universal experience of humanity, turning history into myth and making contemporary
"relevance" permanent.

Notes

1. Quotations from Dickens's letters are from *The Letters of Charles Dickens,* ed. Walter Dexter, Nonesuch Dickens edition (London: Nonesuch Press, 1938).

2. The cover design is not reproduced in the Penguin edition of *Bleak House* but can be found on p. 772 of the Norton edition (ed. George Ford and Sylvère Monod [New York: W. W. Norton, 1977]). Both editions reproduce the illustration that appeared on the title page of the volume edition of *Bleak House,* depicting Jo the crossing-sweeper, and the Norton edition also includes the frontispiece for the volume, which shows the Dedlock mansion in the bare and windswept landscape.

3. *Bleak House,* Penguin English Library series, ed. Norman Page (Harmondsworth, England: Penguin Books, 1971), 941. The notes are reproduced on pp. 936–52 of this edition and repay close attention in relation to the parts of the novel to which they refer.

4. Barbara Hardy, *Dickens: The Later Novels* (London: Longmans, Green & Co., 1968), 14.

5. Philip Collins, ed., *Dickens: The Critical Heritage* (London: Routledge & Kegan Paul, 1971), 272.

6. Ibid., 297.

7. Ibid., 272.

8. Ibid., 273–74.

9. Ibid., 287–88, 276, 285.

10. Ibid., 279.

11. Ibid., 288, 285.

12. Ibid., 287.

13. Ibid., 283, 281.

14. Ibid., 293.

15. Ibid. 298, 275.

16. Adolphus William Ward, *Dickens* (London: Macmillan, 1902), 110–11, 116.

17. G. K. Chesterton, *Charles Dickens* (London: Methuen, 1906), 93.

18. Edmund Wilson, "Dickens: The Two Scrooges," in *The Wound and the Bow: Seven Studies in Literature* (London: Methuen, 1961), 33.

19. George Orwell, "Charles Dickens," in *Critical Essays* (London: Secker & Warburg, 1946), 8.

20. Philip Collins, "Charles Dickens," in *Victorian Fiction: A Second Guide to Research,* edited by George H. Ford (New York: The Modern Language Association of America, 1978), 96. Collins's further observation that the most widely discussed character has been Esther Summerson also provides food for thought. In chapter 6 of this volume I suggest that the Esther of recent readings is a very different figure from that dismissed by Charlotte Brontë.

21. Hardy, *Dickens: The Later Novels,* 16.

22. Philip Collins, "Dickens and Punch," *Dickens Studies* 3 (1967): 23.

23. Humphry House, *The Dickens World,* 2d ed. (London: Oxford University Press, 1960), 33.

24. Ibid. 30.

25. Ibid., 31.

26. Ibid., 33.

27. John Butt and Kathleen Tillotson, *Dickens at Work* (London: Methuen, 1957), 183.

28. Ibid., 184.

29. Ibid., 187.

30. All page references to *Bleak House* are to my Penguin edition.

31. Trevor Blount, "Poor Jo, Education, and the Problem of Juvenile Delinquency in Dickens's *Bleak House,* " *Modern Philology* 62 (1964–65): 328.

32. Quoted by Philip Collins, *Dickens and Education* (London: Macmillan, 1965), 83.

33. I owe this and several other references to Trevor Blount's essay "Dickens's Slum Satire in *Bleak House,*" *Modern Language Review* 60 (1965): 340–51.

34. John Carey, *The Violent Effigy* (London: Faber & Faber, 1973), 31.

35. Information in this paragraph is derived from George Rosen's essay "Disease, Debility, and Death," in *The Victorian City,* ed. H. J. Dyos and Michael Wolff (London: Routledge & Kegan Paul, 1973), 625–67.

36. Trevor Blount, "The Graveyard Satire of *Bleak House* in the Context of 1850," *Review of English Studies* n.s.14 (1963): 370.

37. House, *The Dickens World,* 87.

Notes

38. Philip Collins, *Dickens and Crime* (London: Macmillan, 1962), 8.

39. Ibid., 8–9.

40. Ibid., 235.

41. House, *The Dickens World,* 100.

42. Butt and Tillotson, *Dickens at Work,* 200.

43. Collins, *Dickens: The Critical Heritage,* 283.

44. John Morley, quoted by Jerome Hamilton Buckley, *The Victorian Temper* (Harvard: Harvard University Press, 1952), 5.

45. Orwell, *Critical Essays,* 33.

46. W. J. Harvey, "Chance and Design in Bleak House," in *Dickens and the Twentieth Century,* ed. John Gross and Gabriel Pearson (London: Routledge & Kegan Paul, 1962), 156.

47. Norman Friedman, "Point of View in Fiction: The Development of a Critical Concept," *Publications of the Modern Language Association* 70 (1955): 1180.

48. Jeremy Hawthorn, *Bleak House,* The Critics Debate series (London: Macmillan, 1987), 60–61.

49. Grahame Smith, *Charles Dickens: Bleak House* (London: Edward Arnold, 1974), 8.

50. John C. Ward, " 'The Virtues of the Mothers': Powerful Women in Bleak House," *Dickens Studies Newsletter* 14 (1983): 37. Carolyn Heilbrun's statement is found in her *Towards a Recognition of Androgyny* (New York: Harper Colophon, 1974), 52.

51. Michael Slater, *Dickens and Women* (London: J.M. Dent, 1983), 301–2.

52. Ibid., 304, 307–9.

53. Ibid., 311–12, 356, 363, 367.

54. John Stuart Mill, letter of 20 March 1854, quoted in Collins, *Dickens: The Critical Heritage,* 297–98.

55. Ellen Moers, "*Bleak House:* The Agitating Women," *Dickensian* 69 (1973): 13.

56. Quoted by Slater, *Dickens and Women,* 255.

57. Ibid.

58. *Spectator,* 24 September 1853.

59. Charlotte Brontë's letter of 11 March 1852 is quoted in Collins, *Dickens: The Critical Heritage,* 273. As the date of the letter indicates, she had read only the first number of Dickens's novel, with the opening portion of Esther's narrative, at the time.

60. Slater, *Dickens and Women,* 255–56.

61. Ibid., 257.

62. Hawthorn, *Bleak House,* 58.

63. Michael S. Kearns, " 'But I Cried Very Much'": Esther Summerson as Narrator," *Dickens Quarterly* 1 (1984): 121.

64. W. F. Axton, "The Trouble with Esther," *Modern Language Quarterly* 26 (1965): 545–57.

65. Collins, *Dickens: The Critical Heritage,* 277.

66. A. E. Dyson, "*Bleak House:* Esther Better Not Born?" in *Bleak House: A Selection of Critical Essays,* ed. A. E. Dyson (London: Macmillan, 1969), 272–73.

67. Paul Eggert, "The Real Esther Summerson," *Dickens Studies Newsletter* 11 (1980): 81.

68. K. J. Fielding, "Skimpole and Leigh Hunt Again," *Notes & Queries* 200 (1955): 174.

69. Edmund Blunden, *Leigh Hunt* (Oxford: Oxford University Press, 1930), 258.

70. R. H. Super, *Walter Savage Landor* (London: John Calder, 1957), 406.

71. Blount, 'Poor Jo, Education, and the Problem of Juvenile Delinquency," 338.

72. George H. Ford, *Dickens and his Readers* (Princeton: Princeton University Press, 1955), 111, 130.

73. Alfred B. Harbage, *A Kind of Power: The Shakespeare-Dickens Analogy* (Philadelphia, 1975), xii, 3.

Selected Bibliography

Primary Works

Editions of *Bleak House*

Bleak House was published in nineteen monthly parts from March 1852 to September 1853, with illustrations by "Phiz" (H. K. Browne). Toward the end of 1853 it also appeared in a single volume. The manuscript and corrected proofs of the novel are in the Forster Collection, Victoria and Albert Museum, London.

An important recent edition is that in the Norton Critical Editions series, edited by George Ford and Sylvère Monod (New York: W. W. Norton & Co., 1977).

Secondary Works

Biographies

Collins, Philip. *Dickens: Interviews & Recollections,* London: Macmillan, 1981.

Forster, John. *The Life of Charles Dickens.* London: Dent, 1969. (Originally published in 1872–74.)

Johnson, Edgar. *Charles Dickens: His Tragedy and Triumph.* New York: Simon & Schuster, 1952.

MacKenzie, Norman, and Jean MacKenzie. *Dickens: A Life.* Oxford: Oxford University Press, 1979.

Page, Norman. *A Dickens Chronology.* London: Macmillan, 1988.

Slater, Michael, *Dickens and Women.* London: Dent, 1983.

Critical Studies

Butt, John, and Kathleen Tillotson. *Dickens at Work.* London: Methuen, 1957.

Collins, Philip. *Dickens: The Critical Heritage.* London: Routledge & Kegan Paul, 1971.

Dyson, A. E. *Bleak House: A Selection of Critical Essays.* London: Macmillan, 1969.

Fielding, K. J. *Charles Dickens: A Critical Introduction.* Boston: Houghton Mifflin Co., 1965.

Fielding, K. J. *Studying Charles Dickens.* London: Longman, 1986.

Hardwick, Michael, and Mollie Hardwick. *Dickens's England: The Places in His Life and Works.* London: Dent, 1970.

Hardy, Barbara. *Dickens; The Later Novels.* London: Longmans, Green & Co., 1968.

Hawthorn, Jeremy. *Bleak House* (The Cirtics Debate series). London: Macmillan, 1987.

House, Humphry. *The Dickens World.* London: Oxford University Press, 1942.

Miller, J. Hillis. *Charles Dickens: The World of His Novels.* Cambridge, Mass.: Harvard University Press, 1958.

Page, Norman. *A Dickens Companion.* London: Macmillan, 1984.

Smith, Grahame. *Charles Dickens; Bleak House.* London: Edward Arnold, 1974.

Sucksmith, Harvey Peter. *The Narrative Art of Charles Dickens.* London: Oxford University Press, 1970.

Articles and Parts of Books

Axton, William F. "Esther's Nicknames: A Study in Relevance." *Dickensian* 62 (1966): 158–63.

Axton, William F. "The Trouble with Esther." *Modern Language Quarterly* 26 (1965): 545–57.

Blount, Trevor. "The Chadbands and Dickens's View of Dissenters." *Modern Language Quarterly* 25 (1964): 295–307.

Selected Bibliography

Blount, Trevor. "Dickens's Slum Satire in *Bleak House*." *Modern Language Review* 60 (1965): 340–51.

Blount, Trevor. "The Ironmaster and the New Acquisitiveness." *Essays in Criticism* 4 (1965): 414–27.

Blount, Trevor. "Poor Jo, Education, and the Problem of Juvenile Delinquency in Dickens's *Bleak House*." *Modern Philology* 62 (1964–65): 325–39.

Eggert, Paul, "The Real Esther Summerson." *Dickens Studies Newsletter* 11 (1980): 74–81.

Graver, Suzanne. "Writing in a 'Womanly' Way and the Double Vision of *Bleak House*." *Dickens Quarterly* 4 (1987): 1–15.

Harvey, W. J. "Chance and Design in *Bleak House*." In *Dickens and the Twentieth Century*, edited by John Gross and Gabriel Pearson, 145–57. London: Routledge & Kegan Paul, 1962.

Kearns, Michael S. " 'But I Cried Very Much': Esther Summerson as Narrator." *Dickens Quarterly* 1 (1984): 121–29.

Page, Norman. "Dickens and Speech." In *Speech in the English Novel*, 142–70. London: Macmillan, 1988.

Worth, G. J. "The Genesis of Jo the Crossing-sweeper." *Journal of English and Germanic Philology* 60 (1961): 44–47.

For more detailed listings of Dickens criticism, two very useful sources are *Victorian Fiction: A Second Guide to Research,* edited by George H. Ford (New York: The Modern Language Association of America, 1978):34–113, and *The New Cambridge Bibliography of English Literature,* vol. 3: 1800–1900, edited by George Watson (Cambridge: Cambridge University Press, 1969):779–850. Both listings are by Philip Collins.

Index

Index

About the Author

Norman Page is professor of modern English literature and head of the Department of English Studies at the University of Nottingham, England, and was formerly professor of English and McCalla research professor at the University of Alberta, Canada. He has published over thirty books, mainly on the nineteenth- and twentieth-century English novel; they include *A Dickens Companion* (1974) and *A Dickens Chronology* (1988) as well as a casebook on three Dickens novels and the Penguin edition of *Bleak House*. In addition he has lectured on Dickens and other novelists in universities in many parts of the world, including Spain, Sweden, West Germany, India, and New Zealand. He has held a Guggenheim fellowship and numerous other awards and is a fellow of the Royal Society of Canada.